The Admonitions
of Saint Thomas

to Matthew
the Evangelist

Letters of a sceptic by
John W. McCrum Miller

Printed by The Alpha Xperience,
Newbury, Berkshire

Published 2007 by Drumragh Books,
9 Nuthatch Drive, Reading RG6 5DP

ISBN 978-0-9555728-0-7

To my wife Joan,
without whose patience and support
this book could not have been written.

FOREWORD

This is not a book for the faint-hearted. It will outrage some with its central theory and it will be dismissed as fanciful by others who will demand more 'evidence'. So be it.

What John Miller has sought to address here is both the lack and the confusion of the evidence as we have it for the events leading up to the death of Jesus. To those who will decry the book as pure (or impure!) imagination, one wants to address the question: 'How, then, is the preacher to address the intelligent questioner or doubter?' Shouting ever louder is not really a sensible way of approaching the Thomas of our days; nor is a patronising reassurance that we must simply put our doubts and questions aside.

The painter knows that the sun may be as well depicted by dark shadows on the ground as by a ball of fire in the sky. What Miller attempts in this book is to paint the story of Jesus' last days using a different palette of colours. With long experience as a pastoral preacher and with vivid and arresting use of faith and imagination, we are introduced to a journey of faith and enquiry. The 'answers' provoke more questions and doubts; the journey is in the Way but by often untrodden paths.

I have the great blessing of being able to continue the journey and the quest in conversation with John Miller. The reader is brought into an open discussion where difference is not feared and into a search where fresh eyes are not summarily rejected. I am, myself, a bit of a Thomas (even about this book); I suspect that Miller will be pleased by that!

I commend the book to anyone willing to engage with possibilities before coming to conclusions.

Paul Sheppy, Regent's Park College, University of Oxford

INTRODUCTION

'There are many problems', as one of my earliest teachers of New Testament used to say.

Being brash and callow young students for the ministry of the Presbyterian Church, we barely understood what he meant, let alone believed it. Brought up in the orthodoxy of Ulster Protestantism, which has since attained such a bad name, we knew vaguely that the Bible was to be referred to as 'The Word of God'. Our church life had not been vigorous enough to extend or challenge that expression.

But problems there are, not only with Jonah and his great fish, or with literal interpretations of the Creation story, but within the Gospels themselves. The immense work of Our Lord in sacrificing himself on the Cross for our salvation is in itself difficult to understand, in our non-sacrificial age. Yet it remains, and must remain, at the centre of Christianity, if this faith of ours is to have anything distinctive to offer to the world. I remain convinced of the truth of the crucifixion on Golgotha, outside the walls of Jerusalem about the year 33AD. Others have called this in question (Barbara Thiering: Ahmed Osman). While in no way decrying their efforts, I am concerned about the reader of the New Testament as it stands. If the Cross is to be understood at all in our times, the events leading up to it must be understood also. And events are slippery things. My earliest academic training was in History rather than Theology, so I view the Scriptures with a historical – some might say, historically jaundiced – eye.

The major problems of New Testament criticism which this little work tries to address are not those of language and translation, difficult though these are in themselves. They are the practical questions which a detective, if not a historian, might raise when confronted with the stories as they stand. What, for instance, was the 'custom' by which Pilate released one prisoner at Passover? Why is

Judas Iscariot so universally condemned by the evangelists before, in their own accounts, he has done anything to warrant it? And what exactly did Judas 'betray', if our Lord knew about his plans all along? Turning to the triumphal entry into Jerusalem, who arranged the procession and where did that very opportune donkey come from?

I have not chosen to view the Scriptures through the eyes of Inspector Morse, tempting though that is. Instead, I have chosen one who was of the Twelve, the apostle Thomas. This notorious 'doubter' of the Resurrection seemed to provide a judiciously sceptical pair of eyes and ears, together with a suitably distant memory of the events he describes, to introduce us to the life and times of Jesus. I have chosen the letter format to keep things personal, and to keep them within reach of people whose reading time is nowadays very limited – the commuter on the train, the housewife/husband at the cooker, the last-thing-before-bed tired reader. But I hope that serious Bible students will not take amiss the views here expressed through Thomas, nor my inventions of the centurion at the Cross and of the slave girl. The traditions regarding Thomas, that he went eventually to India and that he was also connected to Edessa (modern Urfa) are both represented here.

An underlying theme is the position of St. Paul in the earliest days of the church, and the relationship of the apostles to him. The earliest books of the New Testament are not the four Gospels, but some of the letters of St. Paul. How did this one-time persecutor of Christians achieve such a pre-eminent position in the Church, so as to be able to dictate its worship, ethics and beliefs to the extent that he did and still does? In the concluding letter I, through Thomas, make an attempt to answer this question. But I shall be happy if the reader, though remaining unconvinced, becomes aware that the question exists.

Both Thomas and Matthew themselves present us with further problems. To take Thomas first. His full title, according to an ancient apocryphal text, was 'Judas Thomas Didymus'. The name Thomas is a transliteration of the Aramaic word for 'twin', which is also the meaning of the Greek word *Didymus*. We may then be fairly certain that his actual name was the common Judas, and that he had a twin sibling: but who was it? The question might be of no importance whatever were it not for the suggestion, again in an early apocryphal text, that he was actually the twin brother of Jesus! To us this would be theologically confusing, to say the least, and I have not adopted it as a worthwhile supposition. Yet the one man who, according to the Gospel, stood out against the resurrection appearance of our Lord in the Upper Room, 'Doubting' Thomas, may well have had his own special relationship with his Master, and I have ventured to reflect this in his account of his time of absence from the disciples and his return to them (see Letter 6). Thomas, as in common with tradition I have called him, was sufficiently well-known in the early church for his name to be used by others who attributed to him spurious works of their own, which have come down to us in the Apocryphal New Testament as *The Acts of Thomas* and the *Infancy Gospel of Thomas*. This practice of false attribution to a well-known author was widely used in order to gain credence for, and give authority to, works which might otherwise have been ignored.

We have still to consider the person and work of St. Matthew, the supposed recipient of these 'Admonitions'. It is generally assumed that he is identical with Levi, the tax-collector whom our Lord summoned from his collecting-table to follow him. It is also assumed that he wrote the Gospel which today bears his name. For the purpose of this work, I have allowed both assumptions to stand. But we should be wary of either. As to the authorship of the Gospel, my remarks about false attribution, above, also apply here. The earliest confirmation of Matthew's authorship comes through Eusebius, who became Bishop of Caesarea in 313AD. In his Ecclesiastical History he quotes the writer Papias as saying, 'Matthew recorded the sayings in the Hebrew tongue, and each interpreted them as best he might.' Papias wrote his work about 130AD, some 200 years before Eusebius. It is not clear what he meant by 'the sayings'. Without going too deeply into what is called 'the synoptic problem' – the problem of the similarities in the first three Gospels, and the differences between them – it is just possible that 'the sayings' were the unknown source-document called by scholars 'Q'. This document was drawn upon by the writers of the first three Gospels, who interpolated its contents in various ways in their own works. If this interpretation of Papias' term 'the sayings' is correct, it leaves the authorship of Matthew's Gospel undetermined. Eusebius again comes to our rescue, however, by stating that Matthew 'committed to writing in his native tongue the Gospel that bears his name.' It is unlikely that so obscure a man as Matthew would have been allocated the authorship of a Gospel without good reason.

And was 'Matthew' Levi the tax-collector under another name? His own Gospel affirms the identity. The name Levi does not appear in either Matthew 9.9 (the call of Matthew the tax-collector) or the list of disciples in Matthew 10.3. Mark, having detailed the call of 'Levi, son of Alphaeus, a tax-collector') (Mark 2.14) finds only a 'James, son of Alphaeus' in his list of disciples, which also includes a Matthew. (Mark 3.16). Luke calls the tax-collector 'Levi' but omits his parentage: and again there is no Levi in his list of the disciples. So, comparing the lists of disciples, we will be fairly safe in assuming that Matthew and Levi were the same person, a tax-collector who gave up that unpopular profession to follow Jesus.

The stained-glass window of St. Matthew by Burne-Jones, which I have used as a prefatory indicator to the Biblical notes, appears by kind permission of the Curator of Ely Museum of Stained Glass. The 'letterhead' of the 'Arms' of St. Thomas the Apostle shows the spear by which tradition has it that he was martyred, and the set-square of his craft as an artisan.

My thanks to the Revd Dr Paul Sheppy, whose ministry at Abbey Baptist Church, Reading, has been a great source of inspiration and encouragement. He has not only read the draft of this work and supplied a Foreword, but has employed his considerable computer skills to supplement my own very meagre ones. Thanks also to Betty Brown for her care in proof-reading. Without her help, the errors would be even more than they are!

John Miller

PRAYER TO SAINT THOMAS THE APOSTLE

O Glorious Saint Thomas, your grief for Jesus was such that it would not let you believe he had risen unless you actually saw him and touched his wounds.

But your love for Jesus was equally great and it led you to give up your life for him. Pray for us that we may grieve for our sins which were the cause of Christ's sufferings. Help us to spend ourselves in his service and so earn the title of 'blessed' which Jesus applied to those who would believe in him without seeing him. Amen.

Internet source.
Prayer Index Page | Catholic Community Forum | Message Board

TABLE OF CONTENTS

Letter 1

In which the Apostle Thomas, having after many years heard from his old friend and fellow-apostle Matthew, encourages the latter in his project of writing down the story of Jesus. Thomas has fled from persecution to Edessa (modern Urfa, in southern Turkey). The year is about 70AD, after the fall of Jerusalem and its sacking by Titus.

To my beloved brother in the Lord, Matthew: grace, mercy and peace.

Glory, thanks and praise be to God, that in His great mercy He has preserved you, safe and well! And that after so many years – can it be thirty already? – I should receive news of you! That such joy should be sent to me in these very troubled times is God's providence indeed! It is my prayer that He continue to keep you safe and well.

Word reached us here in Edessa of the appalling happenings at Jerusalem. We feared for the lives of those of our company left within its walls. All the world knows what butchers these Romans are. We knew that many of our immediate fellowship had already fled before Titus and his army of thugs sealed off the city. But we had no definite word before this of your safety, Matthew, my friend and companion of old. What a joy, and a blessing too, to know you are alive and well.

I suppose that for you as for the rest of us old age is now coming on. Your hand-writing is marvellously firm and clear, so I have hopes that the Lord continues the blessing of good health for you, as he does for me. I have no recent word of any of the Master's friends and our fellow-disciples. Philip I believe is now in Caesarea, spreading the Word wonderfully, and being a light in that dark place. Through him I heard some time ago that Peter, John and Andrew at least were safe. Through them the word of the Master risen from the dead increases mightily. Let the Light shine! Our dear brother James, as you will know, was taken some years ago, and executed with the sword. I have no doubt he died bravely for the Lord, witnessing to the last.

And as you probably are aware Judas – dear, gentle Judas – disappeared from our fellowship altogether, and I hear he too is dead – some say by suicide, others that he had a terrible accident of some sort. I have often wondered about him, pondering what hidden matters he concealed from us all. Such a charming, gentle character, trustworthy above all things. The money, when there was any, never went astray with him! Those weeks of hiding in Jerusalem before the Master was arrested took their toll on him, as I saw at the time. Of course we all lived in fear in those days, in case the authorities might discover our hiding place in that upper room. But it seemed to affect Judas particularly. Strange, when you remember how close he was to the Master.

Now, about your project to write down the story of our journeyings with the Master. You're absolutely right. Since thirty or more years have elapsed since his death and 'rising', his teaching is being quickly forgotten – not so much forgotten as corrupted by false memories! Here in Edessa we have crowds of pilgrims coming to pray at the birth-place of our father Abraham. As I speak with them about the Master, I find the wildest tales circulating. Some say that the Master actually walked on water and stilled storms at sea! Now I know and you know and we all know what we witnessed. We all took part in that first mission when he sent us out in pairs to proclaim the Kingdom. You and I, Matthew, got to know one another better than we had ever done before. I know and you know that wonderful healings were achieved in the power of the Master's name. I cannot and will not deny them, nor will I deny that Jesus the Lord is victorious over death, and reigns with God. As no doubt you will remember, I was the most sceptical of us all when it came to that – but how the Lord blessed my doubts during my time in the desert when I left the fellowship for a while. In fact, this message of the 'rising' from the dead is extremely powerful in spreading the word of the Kingdom here. People seem to understand it at once, and to receive power from it. Followers of Dionysus tell me that this is just what happened to him, but that he confers no power on his devotees – except drunkenness! Greeks point to their god Adonis, who they say goes down to the underworld and rises again. Egyptians say that their god Osiris did the same sort of thing. Their story is that he was hewn in pieces, but then the parts were collected and re-assembled by a goddess called Isis. Mere stories, these, of course – but they point to the 'rising from the dead' of our own beloved Master. When we have proclaimed that, how easy it is to go on to his most blessed teaching about forgiveness, new beginnings in life, and the final establishment of the Kingdom.

A written record would be extremely valuable. Enquirers from all parts of the Empire are clamouring to have certain and sure knowledge of what Jesus said and did while he journeyed with us. Indeed, there are some records already circulating, but they are scanty and in many points inaccurate. Some years ago, I myself wrote down what I remembered of the teachings of the Master: but alas! I lent my notes to someone who never returned them, so now I must rely on memory alone! I have heard that someone called John Mark is also writing an account, indeed may by now have written it. Do you remember him? I don't. There were some very young men who followed with us during the last year or so of Jesus' presence, and it may be that he was one of them. I'm told there are some other written sources which I have not seen. But people are feeling the need for a good, reliable memoir, and you, Matthew would be in a very good position to write it. After all, not many of our company could write at all. Only you and me and John, I think – Oh, and Philip could at least read. But so far as I know, none of the rest could. We were a group of doers, not thinkers. We took what the Scribes told us as true, and committed it to memory. There was no need to write things down till now.

I can copy out for you the sayings of the Master that I remember. Do you think it would be worth your sending me in return a copy of your manuscript? Then I could check it against my own memories, and maybe use it to unlock from my old brain some more forgotten episodes. I know this would mean immense extra labour, but for the Master and his Kingdom one cannot do enough. Perhaps some excerpts from your memoirs would serve to jog my memory – specific teachings, stories, incidents by the wayside.

My one desire in all this is to present and to preserve an accurate record. We are dealing with real people who are genuinely concerned for their salvation. To put before them anything other than the truth would be cruel and blasphemous. There are quite enough rumours, old wives` tales and downright lies already in circulation. Let us set down the truth, in the Master's name.

May he return soon, and bless all who serve him as you do. Thomas.

NOTES AND REFERENCES: LETTER 1

Acts 8 records the 'scattering abroad' of the disciples, not because of Roman attack on Jerusalem, but because of persecution by the Jewish authorities. For whatever reason, the dispersion certainly took place, and turned out to be an effective means of spreading the Gospel.

The sending out of the disciples by Jesus is recorded in Matthew 10, where Matthew himself is in fact 'paired' with Thomas. Another list appears in Mark 3.14-19.

The martyrdom of James 'brother of John' is recorded in Acts 12.2.

There are two accounts of the death of Judas Iscariot: Acts 1.18 says that he bought a field with the proceeds of his treachery, but that he had a fall in it, and 'all his bowels gushed out'. The other, in Matthew 27.5, says that he hanged himself.

The story of Jesus walking on water: Matthew 14.25 and Mark 6.48.

Philip's story is told in Acts 8, particularly 26-40. Azotus, where Philip is 'found', appears to be another name for Caesarea.

Thomas himself, according to one widely accepted tradition, became the Apostle of India, where he was martyred by a spear-thrust. Hence the spear which appears in his crest. A monument said to be his tomb is still extant at Mylapore, near Madras. However, his remains were taken to Edessa, which would seem to indicate a strong connection with that city. But other early sources, including Eusebius, describe Parthia as the scene of his labours, and Edessa, a city in that province, as the place of his death and burial.

Thomas' 'lost notes': A document now known as The Gospel of Thomas was found at Nag Hammadi in Egypt in 1945. Unlike the four canonical gospels, it consists of 113 purported sayings of Jesus, with practically no narrative or context. Its attribution to Thomas rests on one of the few narrative verses in the document, wherein Jesus imparts to Thomas knowledge hidden from the other disciples. See note on Letter 8.

Letter 2

In which two major themes are introduced: the Feast of Purim, and the possible place of 'Barabbas' therein.

To Matthew, beloved brother in the Lord, son of Light and companion of the way, greetings. With all the brothers and sisters here, we continue in prayer that God may strengthen your hands for his work.

I seek your forgiveness, dear brother, for the tardiness of my reply. I can only plead in my defence the very urgent work in the Master's name which comes thronging in upon us daily here in Edessa. As we proclaim Jesus risen from the dead, crowds gather to hear, to question and to enquire. We discuss far into the night, we argue, we pray continually and we praise God together. Our prayers, deep and long, are every day richly rewarded. In my own petitions, your own worthy project has had a high place. And now at last I find a little time to respond to your letter.

We do most urgently need a written memoir. This is becoming clearer every day. Questions are put to us continually: Who were Jesus' family? His wife? Were there children? What did he teach, exactly, on this subject? On that? Above all, we are encountering a thirst for knowledge about the Crucifixion. One might put this down to morbid curiosity, were it not for a consuming desire in the enquirers to know and to possess the salvation that the Master won through his sacrifice of himself. Blessed be his holy name!

But one thing above all others you simply must get across, Matthew, and that is the power of our Master's personality. I know this is asking the impossible! I have never met anyone else whose personal charisma remotely approached his. Do you remember those eyes? One glance into that steady gaze and you had to look away, as if you'd tried to look at the sun. Yet it wasn't horror. No. Not at all. It was more like completeness, fulfilment. You simply didn't need or want anything more. He was simply the most compassionate person I have ever met. When I came anywhere near him, I used to feel 'Royalty' all about me. You knew at once when he came into a room or a group of people, even if you were looking the other way. There was an aura about him, that's all I can say. It was that which got into the sick people, even lepers, and swept away their ailments like dead leaves driven before a storm. I recall Peter telling us once about an experience that he and James and John had when the Master took them with him up some remote mountain. They all three saw him shining with light, transfigured before their very eyes into something like an angel or a sun-god. That sort of thing is hard to believe now, all these years afterwards. But we none of us questioned it then, when the Master walked among us! I believe you should record it.

I always felt, as we walked together from one village to another, as if I ought to be either marching or dancing! I must have shown this on one occasion, because he said to me, with a smile, 'People will think you're drunk, Thomas, if you go along like that!' I'll always treasure that. It's as if I could still hear the voice that said those words to me.

In short, it was as if he incorporated the whole of our humanity in his own person. Indeed, now that I remember, he did prefer to be called 'Son of Man' and often referred to himself by that title.

Beyond that, I think you should put your emphasis on what he taught, and on the great sacrifice of himself. For me the teaching is very important, but the Cross stands out above everything else.

Hideous it may be, but the Cross it is that puts the Master above all other teachers that ever were or ever will be. Far from cancelling out or eclipsing the teaching, it fulfils it. No scribe, no pharisee, no priest, no prophet could ever go as far as that. So emphasize the Cross, Matthew, and the marvel of his appearing again after it. That tremendous personality of his simply could not be destroyed by death.

I hear that John Mark is laying stress on it, but has said that it took place at Passover! A fine concept indeed, and one with strong symbolic associations to commend it: but if my memory serves me at all, not true to the facts. It was at Purim, of that I'm certain. How easy it is to confuse the two festivals, because (as you well know) they fall within a month of each other, and they both celebrate Liberation. But as I remember it, we had come straight from a fellowship supper in the upper room, and gone to the garden called Gethsemane, where we were surprised by the authorities and the Master was taken away. He had planned, I believe, to withdraw to Bethany for a time, while the city filled up with pilgrims for the Passover, which was due at the end of the month. Let me test your memory. Do you remember eating lamb at that last supper together? I don't, and I would have noticed, because I have always been partial to lamb! No lamb, no Passover. It was just an ordinary fellowship meal – though as I now dimly recall, the Master did say some strange things at it. Something about not drinking wine again until he drank it new in the Kingdom: can you remember it more accurately? It's all so long ago that memory plays tricks. But of this I'm sure: it wasn't Passover.

To reinforce this point, I do recollect that our Master almost escaped execution by being appointed the 'Barabbas' for that year. Far removed as I am here from the centre of things Jewish, I cannot remember the full details of the old Jerusalem customs for the feast of Purim. But you know the story behind it as well as I do, how Queen Esther saved our people from being exterminated by the wicked Haman while we were in exile. Her uncle Mordecai was set up in Haman's place as governor, while Haman was hanged. To commemorate this, at the feast of Purim two prisoners were presented to the people, one to represent Mordecai and go free, the other to be executed in the character of Haman. That, as I remember it, was the practice under the Roman jurisdiction.

Of course we never actually executed anyone. That would have been an abomination to us, and in any case, if I'm right, it would not have been allowed under the Roman jurisdiction. But we handed over the chosen victim to the Romans, who had a spring festival which also demanded an execution and a release. At least, that's the way I remember it. Their festival was in honour of the Emperor, and the released one was called by them 'Son of the Father', to signify the rejuvenation of the Emperor's powers, the unbroken continuation of his line. That's how the title 'Barabbas' arose, I believe.

However that may be, I do remember, and remember well, the awful scene outside Pilate's hall of justice, when our Master and another prisoner were produced for the crowd to make their choice. I kept myself well in the background, not wanting to be noticed. But I was all ready to shout for the Master to be released as the 'Barabbas', you may be sure! But, Oh, shame on me! The mob began to shout for the other prisoner! Somehow I dared not open my mouth. There were priests going among the mob, whispering, prodding people to shout for that bandit – for such he was – to be released. Then Pilate asked, pointing to the Master, 'What then shall I do with this one?' And the mob howled 'Away with him to Calvary! Crucify him! String him up like Haman! Crucify! Crucify!' What ghouls they were! I couldn't bear it and crept away in abject silence. I cannot ever forget it. It haunts me still, though I have long known the Master's own forgiveness. Praise be to his name of mercy!

My point, Matthew, is this. All this could only have occurred if the feast was in fact Purim, not Passover. I want to impress upon you the importance of this, and promise to write again about this and other matters. Meanwhile, every blessing attend your work, and may God's wisdom sustain you in all your work for the Master. Thomas.

NOTES AND REFERENCES: LETTER 2

The Jewish Festival of Purim occurs annually in the month Adar, while Passover comes in the following month, Nisan. See the Old Testament Book of Esther, whose sole purpose appears to be to account for the Festival of Purim.

The 'Barabbas' incident is one of the enduring problems of the New Testament. References can be found in all four gospels: Matthew 27.17ff; Mark 15.11ff; Luke 23.18ff and John 18.40ff.

For accounts of the Last Supper, see Matthew 26.17-30; Mark 14.12-16; Luke 22.7ff; all of which connect the meal to Passover. The classic account, however, which forms part of many Communion services, is in 1 Corinthians 11.23ff, wherein St. Paul (who was not present) says it took place on the night of the betrayal of Jesus, and links it indirectly with Passover.

The Transfiguration, in which three disciples ascended a mountain with Jesus, and there saw him surrounded with brilliant light, is in Matthew 17.1-13; Mark 9.2-13; and Luke 9.28-36.

Letter 3

In which Thomas insists on Purim as the Festival at which the Crucifixion took place. He begins to reveal his opposition to Saul of Tarsus, whose reception into the Christian fellowship must indeed have presented difficulties.

To Matthew, beloved brother in the Lord, greeting.

I hasten to send you my good wishes, now that you have actually begun to write your account. May the Lord bless this vital project, and give you light after so many years to set down for all of us a true account of our Master's words and deeds. There is so much darkness, so much corruption, so much decadence in the world. I marvel at the patience of God our Father, that he does not bring the kingdoms of this world to judgement at once! We need light, Matthew, we who count ourselves children of light – and we need it now. So without more ado let me set down an answer – helpful, I hope – to your letter.

But I fear I must begin with a disagreement. You say that you are of the opinion that the Crucifixion of Jesus (I shudder at the very mention of it) took place at Passover. I stand firm in my insistence that it was at Purim. I cannot regard this as a trivial matter, though it seems to come between us at the moment. But it must not and cannot put an end to a friendship as long-standing as ours. The crucifixion of our Master is an appalling event, a horror, whensoever it occurred. It is rendered particularly hideous because it happened to a man as gentle, wise and genuinely good as our Master. But it does matter to get the time right. If it happened at Passover, then the Master's self-sacrifice will be understood to partake of the character of Passover. It becomes a liberation *for Jews only*. It will then be seen as a sign of triumph over others, who, like the Egyptians at the Red Sea, are destined to perish. But this, I insist, cannot possibly be so. I have personally experienced the forgiving love of Jesus our Master, and I know that it can have no limits. I well recall the Master saying that if he were to be 'lifted up' as he put it, he would draw all mankind to himself. But that cannot be so if his sacrifice is seen as connected with a particularly Jewish event like Passover. It becomes exclusive. And this was not the Master's intention; I'm absolutely convinced of it.

You may well reply that for the very same reasons the sacrifice of Jesus cannot be connected with Purim either. Indeed it cannot. And that is why, in the Providence of God, it happened at Purim! Purim is so obscure a festival that nobody outside Jewish circles celebrates it, or knows the story of Esther or anything else about it! You can't make connections with something you don't know anything about. You have to take the sacrifice as it stands, without any tales or myths attached to it. You and I, with our Jewish background, may, if we wish, understand the crucifixion as a Passover sacrifice of deliverance. If we feel that way about it, and derive benefit from so doing, that is our concern. But the Romans, who actually carried out the sacrifice, understood it in quite a different way, and continue to do so. Greeks, Egyptians, Babylonians and others have their own ways of interpreting it, as I keep on finding out when I talk to them. And people in ages to come may find yet other ways which we've never even dreamt of. So I shall continue to insist that it occurred – fortuitously, providentially – at the little-known festival of Purim. And the clinching argument, to my mind, is: *How else could there have been a 'Barabbas'?*

I do not recollect that the Master ever laid any stress on the story of Queen Esther at all. In fact I can't recall his mentioning her in all his teaching, except when we celebrated Purim with him, and, according to custom, he read the story. He did speak about 'liberation' then, but it was liberation from spiritual darkness rather than from oppression. I'm sure he would never have intended and deliberately planned to be crucified in the character of Haman, that wicked, evil tyrant! So it all happened at Purim, *but was not connected to it*. That is my contention. The Master saw his crucifixion as a sacrifice that he had to make on behalf of all mankind – a once-for-all sacrifice that would open the way to God, and it could never be closed again. It shouldn't be connected with any festival whatsoever, not Purim, not Passover, not Hanukah, because if it is, it becomes exclusive. And the way to achieve that was to have it happen at a totally unknown festival, our Jewish Purim. So it was ordained, and so it occurred.

I am seriously concerned as to where all this talk of Passover is coming from, anyway. I've found it in Mark's draft, too. Now Mark wasn't with us for long. I can't remember him at all, myself. Because Purim comes in the month of Adar, only a month before Passover, as you know, the two festivals always ran into each other. Many of the pilgrims coming up to Jerusalem for Passover used to come a month beforehand to fulfil their ritual purifications, which took 30 days, as I recall. So they mingled inevitably with other pilgrims celebrating Purim, and often celebrated it with them. It would be very easy to confuse the two festivals, particularly as they both signified Liberation. That is exactly what young Mark has done, or so it seems to me.

But let me be frank. There is something else that worries me deeply behind all this. I think that that Saul of Tarsus is having too much say in it. Oh, I know he is now accounted 'one of us', and has changed his name to Paul. But I cannot forget what he did to friends of mine in his persecuting days, nor can I forget that I myself am here in Edessa because I had to flee from that persecution. I'm sorry to sound unforgiving, and I know that the Lord can do great things – has apparently done them for Saul. But Matthew, old friend, how hard it is to forgive! The truth is that I suspect, fear and distrust this 'Paul'! My charity is so little, my love so limited. Help me, Lord Jesus: lead me again to the Light. But may I never allow this man, or any other, to pervert the truth of what happened to the Master.

This 'Paul' has indeed said, 'Jesus is our Passover, sacrificed for us.' I've seen it in black and white on a parchment of his that is circulating here. He even goes so far as to give an account of our last supper with the Master, when he wasn't even there! The gall of the man! How dare he infer that, because he understands the Master as some sort of passover lamb, the crucifixion must have been at Passover! To be fair, – I have the document in front of me now – he only says it was 'on the night that he was betrayed' that the supper took place. That is, of course, true as far as it goes. But I do wonder if, with his reputation as a Rabbi, scholar and what-have-you, he isn't over-awing Mark and all the rest of you? He is asserting a quite undue pre-eminence in the church, and I for one object to it.

Now I must leave off, if only to pray for grace to deal with this Saul – I can't bring myself yet to call him 'Paul'. But please bear in mind what I have said about the date of the crucifixion, for the Master's sake and the truth of the gospel.

May wisdom and truth and light from God our father attend you. Thomas.

NOTES AND REFERENCES: LETTER 3

 The escape of Israel from the Egyptians at the Red Sea is recounted in Exodus 14.21ff.

Jesus speaks of being 'lifted up' in John's gospel. See 3.14; 8.28 and in particular 12.32ff.

Mark 14 connects the last supper with Passover.

The persecution of Christians by Saul of Tarsus and his conversion are in Acts, chapter 9.

Paul describes Jesus as 'our Passover' in 1 Corinthians 5.7, and says that the supper took place on the night of the betrayal in 1 Corinthians 11.23ff.

Letter 4

The testimony of Petronius, the centurion in charge of the Crucifixion.

To Matthew, brother in the Lord and son of Light, greetings. Our prayers for you and for your work are being abundantly answered, as I believe this letter will show. I've made what I can only describe as a major discovery in my inquiries about that whole 'Barabbas' business. Among the people here in Edessa there are several old soldiers who know Roman army customs from the inside. God in His Providence has led me to an old man called Petronius, who served his time with the legions, and was actually on duty at the Crucifixion of our blessed Master! He was the centurion in charge of the guard! Now, blessed be Jesus' saving name, he is a convert of ours. When I heard about his experience I sat him down in a tavern and got him to talk about his memories of that frightful day. At first he did not want to say very much, as you may well understand. He still feels terrible about having to play such a leading part in the sacrifice. I doubt if his sense of guilt will ever leave him, despite all our assurances about the forgiveness that is available in that very sacrifice. Now, when the wine in the jug had gone down a good way, he suddenly looked up and said firmly, 'That man ought to have been the Barabbas, for he was truly Son of the Father'. Of course I was all ears, and asked him if he would mind explaining what he meant. When he had finished, I knew I was onto something. I bought another jug of wine at once, asked for pen and parchment, and had him dictate to me a full account. I think he was quite relieved to tell the whole sorrowful story, as I encouraged him to do. So, Matthew my friend, here's a transcript which in my view sheds a flood of light on things.

The Testimony of Petronius,
formerly a Centurion of the XVIth Legion.

'Every year in the army there was a full-dress parade for the Emperor's Birthday. The Emperor, we were all taught, was God. Every man in the army knows that he's also a man, as you and I are men. He grows older as you and I grow older, and eventually goes down to death like any other man. But we had to swear allegiance to him as to a god, who lives for ever. Many of our men came from remote corners of the Empire, where they believe that their rulers must never grow old, or the crops will fail. Look at it this way. The ruling Emperor is God. So he controls the weather, the fertility of the soil, the rainfall, and everything. So he must never grow old or enfeebled and he must never be ill, otherwise the crops will fail. The only way to ensure that is to kill him off while he's still young, and let someone else take on his office as God. In some places in the remoter provinces they still do this. The custom in the army was, not to kill off the Emperor himself of course, but to substitute a prisoner every year who was publicly executed "to take away the Emperor in his weakness" as it was put. That way the real Emperor might continue to reign in strength, and receive the Oath of Allegiance from his manly troops. So every year in the legion we'd get hold of some unfortunate sod, a criminal out of the local jail, or maybe a slave or a beggar. We'd dress him in royal robes as "Emperor", put a mock crown on his head, maybe give him a reed or a stick to hold as a sceptre. Then we'd swear allegiance to him in mockery. Each man had to personally call him names, or spit on him or even thump him. It was part of the drill for all military personnel. Then we'd strip off the robe, put it away in store for next year, and hang the poor devil in public. So the Emperor's weakness was taken away. That was the official line.

'The year I was on Temple duty in Jerusalem, our "Emperor's Birthday" parade coincided with a spring festival of the Jews, called, I believe, "Purim". Their custom at that feast required that two prisoners be released, one to go free and the other to be handed over to us for our purposes and crucified. Governor Pilate had set it up that way, and everyone knew the custom. The one who went free was often called 'Son of the Father' by us, because he stood for a new imperial reign. The Jews called him something else – some name out of their traditions. Governor Pilate allowed the crowd to choose between the two prisoners, which was to live and which to die. The two who were put before the mob that year were both called Jesus. It's a pretty common name among Jews. One was a cutthroat out of the slums; the other was our blessed Master.' (Here Petronius paused, his eyes full of tears. When he had regained his composure, he went on) 'You know how the choice fell out. I think Governor Pilate was doing his best to get the Master off. But the crowd wouldn't have it. The governor eventually gave in, washed his hands ceremonially, and Jesus (now, God forgive me, my Master and Lord) was handed over to us for the annual "treatment".' (Here again he had to break off, and when he continued, it was in a lower voice. The rest of his testimony was punctuated by sobs throughout.) 'I'm so grieved about it now. The whole cohort was paraded, in full dress as usual. We dressed the Master in the robe. Someone plaited a crown out of a prickly thorn bush that grows in those parts, and they jammed it down on his brow with a gauntlet, so that the blood flowed. Then everyone queued up to spit on him or curse him. The centurion – that was me – had to lead off by thumping him or giving him a good crack across the face. Blindfolded and tied as he was, he was defenceless. I stepped up to him, and at once felt an awful restraint I'd never felt before. But I had to hit him, and, God forgive me, I did, hard, on his left cheek. I remember he seemed to turn the other cheek, as if for me to hit him there too. But I couldn't, I couldn't at all. I simply made way for the next man, and found I had to stand with my back to the proceedings because I felt so shattered. When the thumps and curses and spitting had stopped, I knew it was time to take him away.

'The place of execution was outside the walls, quite a way away, because the Jews considered a crucified person accursed, and wouldn't have it done anywhere near the Temple. There were two other victims, thieves I think, who had been passed on to us from other garrison cohorts to "bear away the Emperor's weakness" to the underworld on their behalf. All three were in poor shape, and all three carried the heavy cross-beams on which they were to be nailed. The streets as we passed along were full of people celebrating the feast. They loved to mock the victims going to death, as we had just done. The women were particularly vicious, shedding mock tears and wailing. Some cried "Tammuz! Tammuz! Do not leave us for long! Come back to us, Tammuz!" I didn't understand this at the time, but a man in my cohort who was a Tammuz-worshipper from somewhere out East explained it to me afterwards. This Tammuz was a god of theirs who went down into the world of the dead to revive the spring growth. The louder you wept for him, the sooner he would return.

'I remember this because the Master stopped, and turned to them in a surprisingly dignified way. He even gasped out a little speech, telling them to weep for the things that really concerned them, themselves and their families! I'd never seen anything like this from a broken man going to his death. It came home to me again that this was no ordinary victim. And when his turn came to be nailed to the crossbar, he suffered with such dignity. The first thief was already up there screaming and blaspheming as they all do. But the Master simply gasped, moaned a little, and seemed to pray. We hoisted him up, crossbar and all, onto the upright, and the blacksmith nailed his feet. Then, as he began to squirm and sob, I felt compelled – I don't know quite why – to say, "This man is the true son of the Father. He ought to have been the 'Barabbas', not that other guy." Then we stood watch over the three, to keep the crowd back. They'd come to jeer and make rude comments. Pilate put his usual placard over one of the crosses, the Master's, as it happened. "This one for the Jews," it said. It was an effort to show that he cared for the Jewish people, and was offering this sacrifice on their behalf. Hypocrisy, of course: everyone knew that. Some priests came to gaze: and they were more vicious than all the rest. "Can't save yourself? Too late now!" they said, and laughed at him groaning and helpless up there.

'The Master died early, long before we expected it. He gave a great cry, "My God, why am I forsaken?" and his head slumped forward. One of my men took his spear and shoved it into the Master's rib-cage. Not much blood. His heart had stopped. Best thing for him. The other two hung there till the approach of the Jews' Sabbath put an end to it. Too holy a day for such cruelty, apparently. So we took them all down, bust the legs of the living ones so they couldn't crawl away, and threw them on the rubbish tip for the rats and the dogs to finish off. That, God forgive us, was our way. But the Master's body was spoken for, and some slaves came to collect it. These things I, Petronius, saw with my own eyes.'

Matthew, we must record the Great Sacrifice correctly. Can you make it clear in your writing that it was indeed a Roman sacrifice, for which the Jewish authorities supplied as the victim the man who stood for Haman in their Purim feast? If you decide to use this testimony of Petronius verbatim in your account, I think you'd be better to keep his name out of it. He shouldn't be put down as the man who murdered the Master. After all, he and his men were only following their orders and obeying their usual custom, brutal though these were. I intend to set down for you later the Master's own views, so far as I can be clear about them after so many years.

I have to tell you that I believe I am being guided to move on. My work here for the Master is at a stage when it can be left to others. We have a thriving group of followers of The Way, upheld by the Spirit, as the Master promised. People like Petronius are finding forgiveness, new beginnings and new meaning for their lives. The decadent cultures of the pagans are being challenged and exposed. The Light among us shines more brightly every day. So, as my prayers are answered, I may soon be making a move. There is even a suggestion that I should go to India, to the land which Alexander of Macedon explored. I don't in the least want to go there, but am feeling a strange compulsion towards it, arising I know not how. I understand that it is very heavily populated, and that there are many different beliefs among the people. Anyway, I shall let you know where I go. Your work is too important for me to stand aside from offering what help I can.

May the Spirit bless your continuing labour. Thomas.

Accounts of the Crucifixion appear in all four gospels: Matthew 27.7ff; Mark 15.16ff; Luke 23.26ff; and John 19. The elaborate mockery administered by the soldiers is hard to account for unless it was indeed a pagan ritual, as the centurion above describes it.

The weeping women, and Jesus' response to them, appear only in Luke's account (Luke 23.28ff). The custom of 'Wailing for Tammuz' can be found in Ezekiel 8.14, where the prophet condemns it. While this took place centuries before Christ, there is no evidence that the practice had in fact ceased.

'The Way': Early Christianity appears to have been a movement rather than an organisation. It is referred to as a 'Way' in Acts 19.9, 23.

Letter 5

In which Thomas ponders the miracles wrought by Jesus.

To Matthew, son of Light and brother to all who walk in The Way of Light, greetings. May the blessed Jesus, Light of all the world, shine on your labour in his name.

I have now found time to read what young Mark has written about the Master, giving some account of his outstanding words and wonderful works. This has reminded me of that wild night on the Sea of Galilee when the storm nearly put an end to us all, and we landed eventually on the wrong side of the sea, in the territory called by the Gentiles the Decapolis. My memory of all this is one of calm: the extraordinary tranquillity that surrounded the Master, and which he could impart to people, seemingly at will. Crowds used to stop their babble and hubbub at a gesture from him, so that everyone might hear what he had to say. But that night of the storm was simply astounding. Once we had woken him – and how could anyone sleep, with that tempestuous sea raging? – he simply took command of the situation. I'm no seaman myself, and I confess I felt pretty useless as the boat pitched and rolled and seemed to stand on end amid the foaming combers that came on us suddenly, out of the darkness. But then, also out of the darkness, came that determined voice, 'Calm down, all of you!' followed by a string of commands. 'Simon – steering oar. James, John, Andrew – get the sail down. Nathaniel – baler! The rest of you – two to an oar!' In no time at all he had things organised, and the boat steadied. You would think he had been born to the sea. And everyone was instantly calm, purposeful, re-assured. The storm, of course, turned out to be only a heavy squall, and soon blew itself out, as these things do in Galilee. But afterwards some of us were saying that he even had control of wind and weather! And that, Matthew, is what worries me, because that is the way young Mark (who wasn't there) is describing it. It makes our beloved Master into a mere magician, an abnormal creature quite unlike other men. I admit that I don't trust magicians or soothsayers or anyone else who claims special powers for himself. I've seen too much trickery and deception practised by such people. To class our beloved Master with such charlatans is to deprive him of his majestic humanity. He had charisma. He had quiet authority. Above all, he had compassion. That was what I experienced at first hand on the Sea of Galilee that night. I hope your account will bring this out.

And how strange the day that followed turned out to be! When we finally got ashore, and rested after our ordeal, the Master decided not to go back at once to the Jewish side of the Sea, but to move up a little into this Gentile territory. There was some grumbling at that! Simon the Zealot (remember him?) even said, 'We might meet swine!' The Master reminded him that even swine are God's creatures, and on we went. Not far on, as I recall, we came to a place of tombs. More grumbling: 'Dead people are unclean! Master, why go in there?' And it was there that we met the madman. Remember how he appeared ragged, filthy and raving? Most of our group simply backed away in horror. But the Master showed no fear at all, even when the man screamed at him to leave him alone. Matthew, I do not know how he did it, but in no time at all the Master calmed him down, quieted him, and brought him to a reasonable frame of mind. He pointed to – yes! – a herd of swine which appeared from nowhere. He told the 'evil spirits' to leave the man and go into the swine. The swine at once stampeded and fell to their death over a nearby cliff.

You probably remember all this, Matthew, as well as I do, and certainly better than young Mark. His version has the swine drowning in the sea. As I recall we weren't anywhere near the sea. But what I remember most of all is the fact that the man naturally wanted to join our party, but the Master wouldn't let him! He was told, you probably remember, to go back among his own gentile people and show them what he, the Master, could do by way of healing. I have often wondered, Matthew, how it came about that there were already so many followers of The Way in such places as Damascus before any of us got there. Might it be because that one mad old man who was given a new life spread the word throughout the Decapolis? So it might even be the case that that unspeakable Saul was converted at Damascus because of the madman! Truly the ways of Providence are beyond understanding!

I know I'm reminiscing, Matthew, but to a purpose. In your work you must bring out the Master's compassion. Nobody else could have done anything for that mad old man. Nobody else would approach lepers, as our Master so often did, and with such wonderful effect. Remember how they stank? But he would go up and lay his hands on them. And that woman at the well in Samaria: remember her? You only had to look at her to know what kind of life she led. But for all her lascivious glances he remained utterly unmoved! I do wonder whether the passion that compels men and women to come together was somehow re-directed in the Master, so that it all turned to the sheer power of compassion. Not that he rejected women. Far from it. But he treated them with a respect that I have never seen in anyone else.

I don't know how you will handle this. You must certainly record the mighty works done by our Master. But you must do it in such a way that others may see the glory of his outstanding humanity. What he did, he did as a man: indeed as the 'Son of Man', as all of us well remember. I'm not at all sure that he should be worshipped now, as if he were God. He is our way to God, so far as I am concerned. He provides our only human picture of God. Because he is my human Lord, he is my God. I'm happy to leave it at that.

The followers of The Way here greet you in the Master's name. Thomas.

NOTES AND REFERENCES: LETTER 5

The stilling of the storm and the incident of the Gadarene swine are in Mark chapter 5, with parallels in Matthew 8 and Luke 8.

The woman at the well: John 4.5ff.

For doubt about the worship of Jesus as God, see Matthew 28.17.

Letter 6

Thomas' account of the 'Palm Sunday' entry into Jerusalem, and the part played by Judas Iscariot in it.

To Matthew, beloved in the Lord, Brother in the Light, greetings. You are held daily in our prayers before the great Light of all the world, that he may continue to uphold you by his grace.

I am constantly amazed at the stories about our blessed Master which circulate here. Some of them are so misleading that I fear for the faith of those who hear them. One in particular has come to my notice. People remember our entry to Jerusalem in the Procession of Triumph at Hanukah, but cannot tell why this was done. They will tell me in almost the same breath how our Master once refused to be called King, and fled when a crowd wanted to crown him! Matthew, there ought to be mention of Judas Maccabaeus whenever you write about this episode. Many of our converts here are not of Jewish background, and know nothing of our Jewish history and inheritance. Tell them, Matthew, how some 200 years ago Judas Maccabaeus led our armies to recapture Jerusalem from the infidel, and how he stormed the citadel and cleansed the Temple from the abominations of Antiochus Epiphanes. It's all in the Book of Maccabees somewhere – you'll know where to find it. It was this very Judas Maccabaeus who commanded that we remember his victory every year at the Festival of Lights – and that's exactly what we all did in that

Procession, with the Master gloriously taking the role of Judas Maccabaeus, and going up in triumph to cleanse the Temple. Do you remember how he used the little whip of cords that day? Only a ceremonial whip, of course – not much use if you really wanted to hurt anyone. But he lashed out with it furiously, while the rest of us threw over traders' stalls and chased the owners out! I have to confess that that procession was the most magnificent event I've ever taken part in. I recall saying at the time, 'We're going to certain death along with the Master.' I knew, and I think we all knew, that to come into Jerusalem with such a high hand would be a snub to the priests and a challenge to the Romans. They might find themselves forced to react. Personally, I confess that I feared we would all be imprisoned, or even massacred out of hand. But I had completely underestimated the power of the Master: such a charismatic presence, such wonderful powers of persuasion and command. He simply took over the Temple and controlled it for weeks afterwards, remember? And nobody dared lay a finger on him!

From the moment he mounted the ceremonial donkey to lead the procession, my fears left me, and I began to shout 'Hosanna to the Son of David!' with the best of them. Incidentally, I believe, though I cannot confirm absolutely, that it was Judas (our Judas from Kerioth) who arranged for the Master to have the donkey. Certainly he had the contacts and the money to do it, and everybody trusted him. It could only have been done with the Master's knowledge and consent, which Judas uniquely had. I was worried, I remember, about the Palm branches that people had to wave. I knew as well as anyone that they were the old harvest-palms from the feast of Tabernacles, kept carefully to be taken up at Hanukah – a nice reminder of 'new beginnings', I always thought. But they are a rallying ensign for our Jewish people as well, and I was afraid Pilate and his troops would take our palm-waving throng as an insurrection. I believe there actually was some rioting in the city, quite apart from what the Master and the rest of us were doing in the Temple precinct.

My point in reminding you of it all is this: that we continue to affirm that the Master is a Liberator every bit as great as Judas Maccabaeus, the originator of the Festival of Lights. We are working, as I'm sure you are, in the midst of people with many different beliefs. They worship different gods – not gods at all, of course, but fictitious devils that subvert their worshippers. I am constantly reminded that if I live like the Master, as simply and purely and mercifully as I can, that's what attracts people. The light that shone in him now shines in and through you and me, Matthew, and through all his disciples. But along with that, having the right and true story to tell is what really commands assent. And the Cross is the high point of that story. We must tell that story correctly, Matthew, with all that led up to it and all that came after. It's important, in that context, to proclaim that our Master is Lord of Light, by way of contrast to the darkness of the Cross. Pervert that, even by mistake or forgetfulness, and our mission is doomed to failure in the long term. So I re-iterate: we entered Jerusalem in the triumphal procession at the winter Festival of Lights, doing as Judas Maccabaeus the Liberator ordained, and cleansing the Temple. Someone told me that there are those in the churches who say that even this took place at Passover! Has Saul also been putting this about? At least you won't find that mistake in young Mark's story. We then took virtual control of the Temple during that winter, the Master teaching daily in it and doing a work of great power. The authorities were unable either to confute him or to eject him from the Temple, so popular did he become with the multitude. Then came the season of spring festivals, and they managed to seize him – or rather, he allowed them to do so.

I promised you some memoirs of the Master's own thoughts about his sacrifice. These I shall send as soon as I can find time to collate them. For now, I continue much in prayer about my being called to go to India. A merchant, one Abbanes, has arrived here from one of the petty Kings in that land, looking for a skilled carpenter and stone-mason. My name was passed on to him, and he is now offering me a good wage to go with him to build a palace for his master. Is this, I wonder, a call from the Lord? Pray for me, Matthew, that I may have light in this very troubling matter.

Grace and peace be with you. The brothers and sisters here greet you, and hold you in the Light in their prayers. Thomas.

NOTES AND REFERENCES: LETTER 6

 See 1 Maccabees 4.56ff and 2 Maccabees 10.1-8 for accounts of the re-dedication of the Temple by Judas Maccabaeus. The Feast was instituted in 164 B.C. The practice of carrying palm branches may have come from the autumn Feast of Tabernacles, where Psalms 113-118 were also used in worship, and which also lasted eight days.

Biblical descriptions of what we now call 'Palm Sunday' with the triumphal entry of Jesus into Jerusalem and the expulsion of traders from the Temple can be found in Matthew 21: Mark 11 (the entry only); Luke 19.28ff; John10.22 records that Jesus was in the Temple at 'the feast of the Dedication' in winter time: though he makes no mention of the triumphal entry or of the cleansing.

Thomas' assertion that they were 'going to certain death' arises out of John 11.16.

John 6.15 mentions Jesus' refusal of kingship.

Abbanes the Merchant is mentioned in the apocryphal Acts of the Holy Apostle Thomas (Ante-Nicene Fathers, Vol. 8) as the man who 'bought' Thomas as a slave from Jesus, and took him to serve King Gundaphoros in India.

Letter 7

In which Thomas gives details of his re-conversion to the Risen Christ

Thomas, once a doubter, groping for the way in darkness, but now standing fully in the Light through the victory of Jesus over death: to Matthew, beloved brother in the same Lord, greetings.

What a joy, to receive another letter from you, in these very disturbed times! The package that came with it is an added delight which I look forward to enjoying, as soon as time will allow. How great the Providence of our God, who, though nations reel in trouble round us, has allowed such treasure to survive the journey, and to be delivered here safely by the courier. So now at last, with thanks to God and to you, I receive not only your letter but the precious book of your manuscript notes.

It will take me some time to digest all that you have written about the Master and his teachings. Before I offer any comment on that, I want to offer you something of my own experience, which centres on finding the Master unbeaten by death – indeed, rising victorious over it. If this seems not to be relevant to a factual account such as you propose, I can only say that we need to have something written so that those who read it may believe, as you and I do, that Jesus is Lord. His Kingdom is a present reality. 'The Kingdom here and now' was the burden of all his teaching, as I see your draft manuscript affirms. It is of the utmost importance to get this across to the world. We must also inform those who have already come to faith, and want to know more about the Master.

So I feel myself compelled to write down for you now the thing that matters most of all to me, my experience in finding the Master alive after his crucifixion. It does not form part of the account of his life, I know, but it gave me a completely new life. So I hope it will mean something to you, and through you to anyone who comes to read about it. If, when you've read it, you feel that it doesn't fit in with your own work, please set it aside.

You remember, Matthew, how after the death of the Master in that appalling fashion, we were all dumbfounded, broken, utterly disoriented. Looking back on it, even from this distance in time, I still get the feeling of looking into a chasm, a depth of despair and darkness the like of which I'd never experienced before, and certainly don't want to experience again. Everything I'd hoped for, everything I'd trusted the Master for, was gone, sunk without trace. I'd been watching from a distance as he hung there, though the soldiers kept us well away. I'd seen the spear thrust into his ribs, and known then that he was dead. I must have sat there dumbstruck for an hour or more after they took him down. Then I crept away, and somehow got back to the safety of the upper room. You remember yourself how it was then. One by one people came in, Peter, John, Andrew, James and the others. Nobody said a word. There was a great deal of sobbing, particularly among the women, but not only among them. We felt as if our own life was at an end, as if there was nothing more to live for.

Someone came and said that the body had been put in a tomb, lent by a well-wisher for the time being. The women began to make plans for the anointing, but it was already the sabbath, and in any case none of us dared venture out. That was the darkest, gloomiest sabbath I ever knew.

Then came the mysterious disappearance of the body. First the women came back from the tomb, breathless, and gasped out that the body was gone, the tomb open. Then two of our number, Peter and John I think, ventured cautiously out, and found that this was so: no body, just the grave-clothes lying on the cold stone. I decided to go out to see for myself. It was full daylight by then, and there was nobody around in the garden. It was all very still. I approached the tomb warily, as I recall, not knowing at all what to expect. But there was nothing there. Emptiness. I went right inside, and saw the grave-clothes as the others had said. There seemed nothing for it but to make my way back to the upper room, more dejected than ever. Nothing was left of the Master, not even a grave to weep at. It occurred to me that the authorities must have decided to throw his body on Gehenna, along with the other victims. We'd never find it again, among all that stench and filth, and I wasn't going down there to look.

It was Nathaniel's greeting that took me completely by surprise. Matthew, if there was one person in our group that I found it difficult to tolerate it was poor, dear Nathaniel. Born sceptic as I am, I had no patience for his guileless innocence. Now he faced me with his artless, beaming smile and said, 'We have seen the Master. He's still alive.' I'm afraid I lashed out at him. My grief and pain and confusion just wouldn't allow me to take any more – may God forgive me. 'Nathaniel Bar-Ptolemy,' I said, 'When I see the Master's wounds, and can touch that ghastly spear-thrust in his ribs, I'll believe you!' Then I turned on my heel and walked out. I believe I slammed the door behind me, as I resolved never to return. That's how low I was.

I won't bother you with details of the days that followed. My mind was crazed. All I wanted was solitude, time to think things through, to try to make sense of it all. I hastened away out of Jerusalem to lose myself in the wilderness, just to be alone in the desert. Days and days I must have spent there – something like the proverbial forty! – finding what shade I could from the noonday heat, and shivering at night under the stars. I'll be honest with you: I did think of suicide. A mad scheme came into my mind of climbing onto the highest point of the Temple in Jerusalem, and jumping into the courtyard. That way I would have at least defiled it with my corpse, to spite those loathsome priests. But something held me back. I still wanted to honour the Master, though he was dead. His teaching was still powerful in me: 'Love your enemies', 'Do good to those who despitefully use you', 'I am the life.' So I remained in deep confusion and despair. I knew the old Bedouin trick of sucking a pebble to ward off thirst. I became so hungry that I thought of trying to eat it! Then I became aware that the word of the Master was real, and was still speaking to me: 'I am the bread of life.' In my darkness of soul I was still subject to his direction. The next phase of my wandering is difficult to explain. I wanted the Master desperately. Yet I knew he was dead, so I wanted to escape from him. I saw, as it were, all the kingdoms of the earth open before me. I could flee to any of them, and find a life of some sort free from the whole experience of the Master. I became like Jonah, beginning to know the will of the Master, yet fleeing from it. And bless me if it didn't come back to me: he'd spoken about being like Jonah himself, down in the depths for three days before re-appearing. His words just would not leave me, and I knew for certain that I could never shake him off.

The word of his that finally brought me back to you was this: 'Where two or three are gathered in my name, I am there.' Over and over again I kept hearing it. So finally I knew I must return, and seek out some at least of the old company. I made my way back to the city, and hopefully made for the upper room, although I did not know whether anybody would be there. Can you imagine with what trepidation I ascended the stair, hearing laughter and voices within? Would anyone even recognize me, ragged and unkempt and filthy as I was? I opened the door cautiously, and put my head round it. Oh, what joy to see the whole old company at breakfast! And you were seated exactly as you had been at that last supper! And it was then, Matthew, in that very moment, that I *saw* the Master, seated among you as he had once been! I didn't need to come any nearer. I remember falling on my knees and crying out with relief and joy, 'My Lord! My God!' Then everybody came crowding to greet me, and the vision was gone. But, Matthew, if that was hallucination, I'd rather have it than the hardest of hard reality.

I'm only telling you all this so that, if you wish, you may use it in your work. Whether in writing or by word of mouth, it may help others to believe that Jesus is Lord, that the Kingdom is present here and now, that he has overcome death, and that we may all share in his glory.

I must close now; the time of noonday prayer draws near, and the imperial mail courier will soon depart for Jerusalem. May our loving Lord continue to bless and inspire your work. Thomas.

NOTES AND REFERENCES: LETTER 7

'Nathaniel Bar-Ptolemy': The name-lists of the twelve disciples given in the four gospels do not tally. Nathaniel only appears in the list in John, but Bartholomew is absent. It is conjectured that Bartholomew is a corruption of the surname Bar-Ptolemy, and that the two names therefore belong to one man, as they are presented above.

The name Thomas itself presents a difficulty, since it means 'a twin' (see Introduction). Speculation has arisen that he may even have been a twin brother of Jesus: though the well-known stories of Jesus' birth would seem to contradict this. However, *The Gospel of Thomas* includes a saying attributed to Jesus that 'whoever drinks from my mouth will be as I am, and I myself will become that person......' Elaine Pagels has suggested in *Beyond Belief* that Thomas may thus symbolically be seen as a 'twin' of Jesus.

With that in mind, I have ventured in the letter above to suggest that Thomas' experience in the 'desert' of separation from the other disciples paralleled that of our Lord, whose temptations in the desert are recounted in Matthew 4.1-11 and Luke 4.1-13.

Letter 8

In which Thomas queries Matthew's allusions to the Old Testament to support his narrative: in particular calling in question the virgin birth.

To my beloved brother Matthew, greetings in the Lord of Light. May the prayers of all companions of the Way surround you, as ours continue to do.

May I offer a tentative comment on your idea of attaching the stories of the Master to appropriate sayings from the Prophets and the Psalms? It is – at first sight – very appealing. It should, as you say, attract many who share our Jewish outlook to consider the Master as the Messiah. How we learned to long for his coming! How earnestly we sought in the Scriptures for promises from God that He would soon send the Messiah-Liberator to his people! I do indeed believe that the Master is that Messiah, as you and the rest of our brothers and sisters do. But Matthew, forgive me for raising a little doubt – you know me of old! If you attach any given episode of our Master's life to some quotation from our Scriptures, is there not a danger that you might, even unintentionally, re-write the episode to suit the quotation? I am aware that this is a fashion of writing that is highly regarded among our scholars. But, Matthew, is it – how shall I put it? – true to what actually happened? For instance, you could have an event in the Master's career – and it is a very long time ago – which

37

you remember only in part. You find a Scripture that reminds you of the event. Then you record the event as happening to fit that particular text, and *not* as it actually occurred. I hope I make myself clear. It is of the utmost importance that we set down the Master's thoughts and deeds as accurately as we can, now that so many of those who knew him in the flesh are dying away. Forgive me for saying all this, but even a writer of your learning and diligence may be misled.

I have an example in mind. You tell me you are proposing to include some stories about the birth of the Master. I confess I am a little reluctant to enter into this, because, as you may remember, my own twin brother remained unknown to me. All I was ever told about him was that he had been fostered out, as my parents were too poor to keep him and me together. I mentioned this to the Master shortly after I joined the group. Seeing that I was deeply troubled by this, as I had been for years, he honoured me by saying that I could be his own 'twin' if I liked! It was then that he gave me the nickname 'Thomas', which has stuck with me ever since! He had a depth of understanding which I have never seen surpassed. But as to his own childhood, I don't remember his ever saying much about his home life at all. I know he was a carpenter by upbringing, and I can vouch for that, having practised the trade myself. I always assumed that his father must have been a carpenter too, to bring him up to it. Also, it was put about that there was royal blood, blood of the house of David, somewhere in his ancestry. If that is true, it's extremely important, because it fits in with our Jewish expectations of the Messiah. But now, would you believe it? Some people in our church here are circulating a wild tale that his mother Mary remained a virgin till the day of her death! I believe they get this preposterous idea from pagan stories of foreign gods, who were supposed to have been born in all sorts of strange ways. Adonis, for instance, came, they say, from a split myrrh-tree! Venus, a goddess of the Romans, simply rose out of the sea! Dionysus was born from the thigh of his father! I discount all such tales as fantasy. They do nothing for the credibility of their heroes, indeed they detract from it. I know as well as you do what precedes birth. A woman cannot both have a child and remain a virgin. It might be said that I'm setting my little human experience and knowledge before the power of Almighty God. Be that as it may, I have to go by the light God gives me, and that light shows quite clearly that female virginity and motherhood cannot possibly go together.

I feel I must mention this to you, because somewhere in Isaiah there's a saying of the prophet about a young woman bearing a son to be called 'God With Us'. You will know the passage I mean. Our scholars have insisted that this is a foreshadowing of the Messiah. I have heard some say that this young woman was to conceive without the intervention of a man. But that cannot possibly be a correct interpretation. Isaiah would have been laughed to scorn if he had said any such thing! I remember checking up on that saying when I was young and gullible, and finding that Isaiah did indeed say 'a young woman', not 'a virgin'. Whatever you do about the birth-stories of the master, Matthew, don't be beguiled into including that text! People might deduce from it that if his parenthood was in some way different from any other, then he himself could not have been fully human. Besides, if he had no ordinary human father, what becomes of his descent from King David? If I remember aright, he said his father's name was Joseph. He came from Nazareth.

I'm sorry to insist on this at some length. I don't want any misconception – a good word, you'll allow – to grow up around the Master. He was always so down-to-earth, so realistic about life. I sometimes think he was the only truly 'human' being among us. In his company, I often used to feel completely inadequate, only half the man God meant me to be. I knew the meaning of 'Sin' as I never knew it before. But I also knew that he would go to any length to rid me of that sin, and make a true man of me. Oh, the sheer Majesty of the Master's presence! The vast embrace of his compassion! I don't know if you and the others felt like that. But I remember still that it was a great relief to you to get rid of that tax-collecting business.

How relieved you were when the Master re-assured that little man who climbed the tree – was his name Zacchaeus? A tax-collector anyway, and the Master didn't shun him or reprove him.

Before I close, I want to add something about the last days of the Master. I remember that he set his mind resolutely to go up to Jerusalem. We were all against that plan, right from the start. For one thing, we had acquired such a following round Capernaum and in Galilee that we thought he should be content with that. We all were. Furthermore, we all knew that the priests and scribes in Jerusalem would oppose us tooth and nail. Indeed, I was afraid that we would all be imprisoned, perhaps even executed. Remember those long talks at Caesarea Philippi, when he began to teach about the Servant of the Lord and the sacrifice he had to make? There was a stand-up row with Peter about that, do you remember? But that teaching is so important, Matthew! Please do it full justice when you come to write about it. My memories are of the hiding place in the upper room, and of looking over my shoulder all the time to make sure I wasn't being followed by any spies of Caiaphas. It wasn't an easy time, those last weeks in Jerusalem. The Master longed to stay there till Passover. But we only held out until Purim before the Master was arrested.

I'll write again. My preparations for moving on are taking shape. Despite all my misgivings, the Master is pointing me more and more firmly in the direction of India. Whatever the outcome, I plan to leave here in the near future. I'll keep you posted as to where I am.

Grace to you and peace. Thomas.

NOTES AND REFERENCES: LETTER 8

 The virgin birth of our Lord is found in Matthew 1.18ff; Luke 1.26ff gives the visit of an angel to Mary to announce the forthcoming birth.

The prophecy of 'Immanuel' appears in Isaiah 7.14.

Jesus' conversation with the disciples at Caesarea Philippi appears in Matthew 16.13ff and Mark 8.27ff.

The incident involving Zacchaeus is in Luke 19.1-10. St. Matthew does not in fact record it.

On the name Thomas, see Introduction.

Letter 9

In which an incident from the Gospel of Thomas *is the main theme.*

Thomas, Servant of the Master at the fountain-head of faith, the very birth-place of Abraham: to the beloved Matthew, greetings in the name of the Lord Jesus.

I fear you will want to take my greeting with a pinch of salt! I'm encouraged by your response to my letter about my personal experience of seeing the risen Master, to reveal to you something even more personal. I may have my doubts about the cave here in Edessa being the real birth-place of Abraham (you know my sceptical nature!) but I do claim that my experience of the Master is authentic. So I shall endeavour to set it down, exactly as I remember it.

The Master once took me aside, and enjoined on me a most surprising thing. He said that prayer, fasting and works of charity might damage my spiritual life, and that I should be very wary of them! At the time, he said I should not tell the rest of you about this, because it would have been too unsettling for you. Indeed, he warned me that I might be stoned for blasphemy by the rest of you! So I still feel I'm taking something of a risk in setting this down. But you must make of it what you will. I'm old now, and feel that if the truth gives offence, it's a pity, but I can live with it. However, let me try to explain what I think the Master meant.

42

Do you remember a time when he gathered us all together, and asked us what sort of person we thought he was? I remember feeling very uneasy at the question. Only he himself could possibly answer it. Should we compare him to a teacher, a scribe, a healer – what? Peter was the first to venture an answer. 'A prophet, a very righteous prophet.' Something like that was his suggestion. Then there was a silence while we all thought about it. Someone else – could it have been you? – spoke up. 'A very intelligent man, a lover of wisdom.' We all pondered this for a bit. I thought to myself, 'That's good. Wisdom is God's own instrument for creating the world. The Master is always talking about the Kingdom which he is creating.' But I still wasn't satisfied. There simply wasn't, and still isn't, any human category into which I could dream of fitting the Master. So I resolved to say so. 'Teacher,' I began, 'I don't have an answer ...' But of course I had called him 'teacher', so he took me up on that! 'I'm not your teacher!" he said firmly. "You're talking like a drunk! You're already intoxicated with what I've been sharing with you.' Then he took me aside, and gave me that strange command, not to pray, fast or give alms lest it destroy me. In fact, he said that to anyone who was as deeply immersed in the Kingdom as I already appeared to be, these three religious rituals would be unnecessary. When we returned to the rest of you after that wonderful private audience, I took his advice and would not reveal anything that he'd said to me. I'm sure you can understand why.

Let me immediately confess that I do still pray, fast and give alms. Since the Master went before us, I no longer feel as close to him as I used to in the days of his presence, and I do find those three customary disciplines helpful. But I hope that one day, when the kingdom has come fully and finally, and we are returned to God's paradise as it was in the beginning, the disciplines of religion will indeed all fall away. They won't be necessary any more.

Matthew, I don't know if any of this very personal reminiscence will fit in with your narrative of the Master's days with us. If it does, you're perfectly free to use it. If not, please feel equally free to forget it.

43

Another big group of pilgrims has just come in, seeking the birth-place of Abraham. Pray that I may be enabled to show them the way to the very beginning, the paradise of God restored! May he that is all Wisdom bless your labours. Thomas.

NOTE ON *THE GOSPEL OF THOMAS*

In 1945 an Egyptian peasant searching for fertilizer at the base of a cliff near the village of Nag Hammadi, unearthed a large sealed pottery jar which lay buried in the sand. Inside it he discovered a collection of twelve very ancient writings. These had been hidden in the jar, possibly by a monastic community who desired to keep the documents safe, either from vandals or even from the church authorities themselves. For the writings, when examined by scholars, proved to be sources of Christian teaching which were in many cases so different from our current New Testament as to call the canonical gospels into question. Among them was a short document containing only sayings of Jesus, and beginning, 'These are the hidden sayings that the living Jesus spoke and that Didymus Judas Thomas wrote down.'

Thus *The Gospel of Thomas* is in fact not a gospel at all, if by that term we mean a continuous narrative of the life, work and words of Jesus, as in the four 'canonical' gospels. It is simply a list, and a very short one, of sayings attributed to Jesus. For all its brevity, it has been described by Stevan Davies as 'the most important manuscript discovery ever made' to any who are interested in Jesus and his teaching. It confirms that many of our Lord's sayings, recorded in the New Testament, were also recorded elsewhere, and by other hands than those of Matthew, Mark, Luke and John. New Testament scholars have long accepted the existence of an undiscovered 'Q', a primary source-document from which Matthew and Luke alike drew portions of their material. The discovery of The Gospel of Thomas confirms that there were indeed such sources, and that they put a different 'slant' on some of the central teachings of Jesus. For example, where the canonical gospels emphasis a Kingdom of God yet to come, 'Thomas' stresses rather the concealed presence of the Kingdom now.

Jesus said: 'If your leaders say to you "Look! The Kingdom is in the sky!" then the birds will be there before you are......Rather, the Kingdom is within you and it is outside of you. ....If you do not know yourselves, then you exist in poverty and you are that poverty.' ....Jesus said, 'Recognize what is right in front of you, and that which is hidden from you will be displayed to you.' (*Gospel of Thomas*, sayings 3a and 5: Stevan Davies).

The seed is already in the ground. Look within yourself to find Light and discover Truth. Contrast this with St. John's gospel, wherein it is claimed that Jesus alone is the Truth and the Light of the world.

It has been suggested that one of the reasons why *The Gospel of Thomas* was excluded from the accepted Canon of Scripture was indeed that it placed spiritual 'Light' within the believer rather than having it externally supplied by Jesus.

His disciples said to him: 'Show us the place you are, for it is essential for us to seek it.' He responded, 'He who has ears, let him hear. There is light within a man of light, and he lights up all of the world...' (*Gospel of Thomas*, saying 24: Stevan Davies)

Hence in these letters, Thomas' constant references to 'Light' and 'Children of Light' in a manner more redolent of Buddhism or Hinduism than might be thought fitting in today's Christianity.

As to date, *The Gospel of Thomas* falls in or before 62AD, the date of execution of James 'the Just', who is mentioned by name in the text. He was a brother of Jesus, not to be confused with James, brother of John, who was martyred earlier.

Letter 10

Thomas remembers Jesus' teaching about his sacrifice, based on the 'Servant Songs' of Isaiah.

To Matthew, Son of Light, brother beloved in the Lord Jesus, greetings. I pray always that you may continue in health, as by the mercy of God I do myself.

Your latest letter took some time to reach me, as I have now begun my journey southwards. My decision about India was finally resolved for me some time ago, as I reflected that I am a slave, bought with the Master's blood, and that a great kingdom is waiting there to be illuminated with his light. We are light-bearers, Matthew. All of us who knew him bear his light. Did he not say something once about not hiding light, but putting it on a lamp-stand? The lands to the East, under the rising of the sun, compelled me more and more, and now I have consented to go. But I shall be in this town for a few months now, as the passes through the mountains are blocked. They always are in winter, so I shall be here for three months at least.

My journey so far is proving very profitable in the Gospel, as many hear of our Master's rising from the dead, and seek me out about it. It's the taking away of sin and *imperfection* that impresses them, as well it might. I've underlined 'imperfection' because it has come as a new idea to me. People coming here from India seem to stress it in a way that the Master also did. He shocked me when he demanded that we become 'perfect, as the Heavenly father is perfect'. There is indeed the assurance of completely new life in the Master – how powerful that is, and with what delight men and women receive it! They have never found this in their own teachings, so I strive to instruct them as best I can.

I promised to set down for you the Master's own view on his sacrifice, as best I could remember and understand it. One of my deep regrets is that none of us thought to write these things down while the Master was with us. I made a futile attempt to take some notes once, but I lost them – alas! Like everyone else, I didn't want to miss a word of his, and in any case the teaching about sacrifice was so new and shocking that it left me, at least, nonplussed and dumbfounded. As I recall, he took words of the prophet Isaiah about a 'Servant of the Lord' who should suffer and die to take away the sins of the people. Our teachers always said that those passages referred to the whole people Israel, and explained the sufferings we as a people had undergone and would still undergo, as being a sacrifice for the nations of the world. It used to make sense to me in my boyhood days, because our people have suffered so much from persecution. Assyrians, Syrians, Greeks, Egyptians and now Romans – it has never stopped. We've been exiled, and bounced back from that. We have been bullied, oppressed, enslaved – but still by a miracle of grace we live on, praising the God of Israel. Isaiah saw what was happening in his own time and wrote that the Servant-People have to undergo conspicuous suffering, so that other nations, seeing it, might know the power of God to raise his people up again. We couldn't have done it ourselves – that was the argument – so our God did it for us. Therefore the nations of the world would in due time come to worship our God in Zion. They would set aside their own gods, with their decadent and disgusting worship, and be healed into new humanity.

I had understood it in this very orthodox way, until the Master began his teaching at Caesarea Philippi. He applied it all to himself, and that really was a blinding revelation. Isaiah and the other prophets had indeed spoken of Israel as being reduced to 'a remnant'. But the Master reduced that 'remnant' to just one man – Himself! That left me astounded beyond measure. I just sat there, not uttering a word. Then he went on to explain that this meant he himself must suffer. 'By his stripes we are healed', 'he was bruised for our transgressions, wounded for our iniquities' – Isaiah's famous poem that we all had to learn as boys came tumbling out with a new, terrible and immediate, meaning. He was going to die. I knew it before he said it. And when he did say it, I knew someone would explode. It had to be Peter, of course: Peter, the very man who, I think, had said that the Master was the Messiah only an hour before! But Peter's heart is in the right place, even if his temper does run away with him sometimes, and he took the Master's anger in good part eventually.

There was a great deal more to the Master's teaching about sacrifice. 'The sacrifices in the Temple at Jerusalem are not perfect': that, I think, was his argument. 'To make them perfect, there would have to be a perfect victim and a perfect high priest to offer it.' I remember thinking at the time, 'That sounds like something the Greeks would say', but I held my tongue. He went on to talk about the way parents will make sacrifices of another kind. A mother will put aside money she can ill afford to send a child to a good teacher. To get a doctor when a child is ill, even a Roman will swallow his pride and go to a Jew – remember the centurion who came to us when his daughter was ill? People know how to make sacrifices for love's sake, and so does God, the Father of all. That was the gist of his teaching, that God would give even a son of his, well-beloved and well-favoured, to save his people from their evil ways. That Son, a perfect specimen of manhood, would be spurned and killed by an evil people. But once he was dead, they'd see what they had done, and return to God in penitence. If they failed to see that Son's glory in his death they would be lost to all humanity. But people of other nations who saw his death and repented would take their place as

God's people on earth. Something like that is the way it ran, Matthew, and what I teach is along those lines. A perfect life, perfectly offered in public sacrifice to God, draws all sorts to it. If we preach the Cross, people take sides with the Master and want to embrace his ways. They find their sin put away, and new life made possible.

As well as this, there's the teaching about loving and forgiving even your enemies. I never heard anyone else teach like that. Jesus the Master said it with such authority: 'Forgive infinitely, without limit. Even seventy times seven isn't enough.' I remember thinking, 'But that's impossible.' Then I had to correct myself. 'That's impossible without God's help.' Again, 'If God has forgiven me, and I am absolutely certain that He has done so, then I can have strength to forgive others.' That comes in the Master's prayer-method, doesn't it, only the other way round, 'Forgive us, even as we forgive others.' At first when I heard it I said within myself, 'That means we shall be trampled into the dust by every egotist that comes along.' But as he went on teaching about turning the other cheek to the smiter, and going the second mile when a soldier of the occupation force compels you to carry his pack for one mile, I began to see that this was a whole new way of life that he was offering. It is in fact a new way of looking at things that stops violence in its tracks. Otherwise blow leads to blow, insult leads to insult, and the situation deteriorates into bloodshed.

That, Matthew, is how I remember his teaching at Caesarea Philippi, while the beautiful clear waters of that spring went rippling past on their way down to the Jordan. Such clear, refreshing water of life! Such sombre teaching, but so life-giving!

Speaking of hatred brings to mind something I'd rather not remember, but cannot keep back from an old friend like you. There was one man in our group I could never get on with: Nathaniel. Perhaps you realized that, though in deference to the Master I did my best to hide the fact. Brotherly love has to be striven for sometimes! One particular incident came to mind the other day, as I was talking to one of our converts about raising a dead person to life. Do you remember Lazarus of Bethany? How the Master got him out of his tomb alive, though they'd buried him as dead? When the Master first heard about his 'death' he said at the time that Lazarus wasn't dead at all, but that it was some kind of deep sleep, and that he, the Master, would go and rouse him. I recall the thrill that that gave me, and I said something like, 'I wish we could all die with him', to which Nathaniel (bless him!) replied, 'Trust you to talk about dying!' He'd completely missed the point! I meant, of course, that if only we could all 'die' in that manner, we would all be privileged to hear the Master's voice calling us out of the tomb to new life. I was never nearer an open quarrel with Nathaniel than at that moment – but I held my tongue for the Master's sake. And now, praise be, I know that death, which can't be all that far away, will be only a sleep from which the Master will indeed call us all. For he has passed that way himself.

I seal this letter in the hope that its contents may be of some assistance. The teaching about sacrifice is essential, and will I am sure find a place in your memoirs. All glory to the Master, who perished on the Cross for us all. Thomas.

NOTES AND REFERENCES: LETTER 10

Isaiah 53 is the key passage on vicarious suffering.

Jesus' teaching on forgiveness; Matthew 18.21; Luke 17.4.

The raising of Lazarus: John 11.

Jesus' teaching on human perfection; Matthew 5.48.

Letter 11

In which Thomas remembers the cleansing of the Temple at Jerusalem, and the role played by Judas Iscariot as a go-between for Jesus with the authorities in Jerusalem.

To Matthew, beloved brother in the Lord Jesus, greetings. With all the companions of the Way I pray that God may give you wisdom and light as you set before mankind a memorial of the Master.

As you tell me your labours are now well advanced, I must hasten to set down more of my own memories of our dear Master – may he soon return! Why does he so delay his coming? I recall his saying to me, 'Blessed are those who have not seen, and yet believe.' How blessed our new believers are indeed! They came from darkness into light, as they joyfully proclaim. They emerge from shadows to the glory of the day.

To business. I will now set down for you some views of my own, which you may or may not find helpful. I hope they are, and that you may be able to include at least some of them in some way. About the great Sacrifice. Our master was perfectly clear at Caesarea Philippi. He was going to make of himself the victim in a sacrifice which would atone for the sins of the whole world, and so, in the end, render all other sacrifice unnecessary. I recall thinking at the time, 'How can this be? Human sacrifice is an abomination! Our good Jewish law would never countenance it! Can it be that he will put himself in the hands of pagans, among whom awful things are done as acts of worship? Will he make of himself an offering to pagan gods?' I wish that I had asked him about this at the time, but my musings were too inchoate for that. Besides, I feared the mockery of the others. I could just hear Nathaniel – that dear, guileless idiot Nathaniel! Whatever happened to him? – saying, 'There's old Tom, asking questions again!' So I held my tongue. But in my heart I knew that a human sacrifice in Jerusalem was practically unthinkable. How could such a monstrous thing ever be envisaged, let alone arranged and actually carried out? It began to come in on me even then, while the Master was expounding a portion of Isaiah to us, that the Romans would have to be involved. Someone would have to act as a go-between for him with the Romans in Jerusalem. If he tried to arrange this appalling thing himself, they'd either laugh him to scorn or think he was too dangerous to handle. After all, no one in his right mind would offer himself for ceremonial slaughter. They take a slave or a prisoner or some ne'er-do-well and use him.

Then I began to think, who among us could act discreetly to get our Master put into the hands of the Romans to become the victim in a ceremonial sacrifice? Though my whole being felt revulsion at the very idea, yet I found myself at the same time compelled to think along these lines. It was a very strange sensation – thinking of something I did not want to think of, regarding a situation as both preposterous and inevitable at the same time! Amid the turmoil, the one who came to mind was Judas – our dear, trusty, reliable Judas. He had contacts, we all knew that, with all sorts of people, Jews, gentiles, Greeks, everybody. If money was needed to grease a palm here and open a door there, he had it. I didn't then know about our Master's own network in Jerusalem. Those Qumran people were so secretive. But in any case they were practically all Jewish. Judas had access to influential people. And the Master trusted him absolutely.

It also became clear to me at Caesarea Philippi that there was going to be strong resistance in our own group to going up to

Jerusalem at all. Peter, of course, spoke up, and got fiercely put down for it. But he stood for the rest of us, including me. If we thought he would die in Jerusalem – and I for one thought it was suicide for him to go near the place – then we wouldn't let him go! In fact we planned, don't you remember, to dig our heels in and refuse to go with him on such a madcap adventure! We told him the priests would have him stoned to death for blasphemy, and where would be the sacrifice in that? But it was impossible to resist the Master when he had set his mind on doing something. He just went on regardless.

He started the journey towards Jericho, and we all thought, 'Jericho. That's all right. We'll go as far as that and no further.' Then – remember – he heard that Lazarus of Bethany was ill. To appease us, as I now see it, he delayed a day or two before going to a place so close to Jerusalem: but he went in the end. Now that I think of it, he did say that his 'hour' had not yet come. I wonder if he meant that the arrangements that Judas was even then making in Jerusalem were not yet finalised? Do you remember whether Judas was with us from Jericho on? I don't recollect seeing him. Hanukah was approaching, and we all thought, 'He'll try to get to the Festival of Lights. No sacrifices involved there. We might just be all right at the Festival of Lights.' But then we heard that he was arranging through Judas to ride the ceremonial donkey, and play the part of Judas Maccabaeus liberating the Temple! We were all caught by surprise with that. The prospect of making an entry to the Temple itself in ceremonial triumph went some way to allaying my fears. But I still felt a curious foreboding as the day approached.

Well do I remember how I felt as the customary procession assembled at the Mount of Olives, the crowds bringing their old harvest palms, and the sense of expectation as we saw the two men approaching up the hill with the donkey in its ceremonial harness! The man leading it was indeed Judas, and straight to the Master he brought it! The shouts of 'Hosanna to the Son of David!' began to rise, and I could scarcely believe either my eyes or my ears! I'd pictured us slipping into Jerusalem quietly and lying low so as not to antagonise the authorities. But not a bit of it! Here was the Master making the most high-profile entry he could devise, and Judas had helped him do it! We started out in high delight, all trepidation put aside, down the Mount of Olives, across the Kidron, and on up by the traditional route to the Temple. I confess my 'Hosannas' were a little bit muted as we passed in to the city under the gateway, and surged on up towards the great Court itself, the 'conquering hero' coming to claim his own. By the time we got there, my doubts had vanished, and I was bawling as lustily as anyone, 'Blessed is he that comes in the name of the Lord!' Then the master produced that fly-whisk thing that was used on Liberation day, (I wonder did Judas arrange that too?) and proceeded to lay about him with it. If that was supposed to be a merely ceremonial 'cleansing' of the outer court, it turned into a near-riot, if you remember. 'Unceremonious bundling-out' would be a better description of what happened, and no doubt you'll put that in your account. The traders, the pigeon-sellers, the Annas Bank people that used to change money into 'pure' Temple coinage with no image of Caesar on it – out they all went neck and crop, and didn't dare to come back! Then the master simply took over the Temple for the entire duration of the Festival of Lights. He preached to the crowds, he answered questions, he quarrelled openly with the priests and scribes when they started to object. Honestly, I was afraid at that time that we'd all be landed in prison. But how well the Master held his own! Get that in, Matthew. And how well someone (Judas again?) had arranged for us to have a safe house to hide in! I'd hoped that once Hanukah was over we'd slip out of the city and get away back to Galilee again. But of that there was never the slightest hope! Once the Master was installed in Jerusalem he wasn't going to leave it again before Passover, and that was three months away! So I began to think, 'He's got us in here, and he'll get us out', and I got quite resigned to lying low in the 'Upper Room' at least till Passover. You remember how he said he was longing to have Passover with us in Jerusalem? But he went on preaching in public, and nobody dared lay a finger on him.

Judas – to get back to him – was still being the go-between, I believe. He was fixing that at Purim, a month before Passover, the Master would actually be taken into custody, so that he could be presented to the crowd as a prisoner. They would naturally want to exalt him as the 'Mordecai' of the festival, while some other poor sod got sent down for execution as the 'Haman'.

That, Matthew, is my considered view of it, with hindsight. But of course it all went horribly wrong, from our point of view: and, I think, from Judas'. After what actually happened, Judas wasn't ever able to forgive himself. He felt a terrible guilt about it, as you can well imagine. He was such a close friend to the Master! He never once betrayed the location of our upper room, and I'm sure it was never his intention to betray the Master at all. He had to arrange a quiet arrest, and he did it with the Master's full knowledge and approval. In fact, I do remember somebody telling me that at our last meal together the master actually said to him, 'Do what you have to do now, and do it quickly.' Anyway, that's my opinion, Matthew. Make of it what you will. Poor Judas – poor, poor Judas!

Must stop now. A new camel train has just come in from the South, and there's a rumour that the passes may be open. I'll keep you posted as to where I am. Peace be with you. Thomas.

NOTES AND REFERENCES: LETTER 11

Nathaniel is described as 'guileless' in John 1.47

Jesus' determination to go to Jerusalem; Luke 9.51.

The 'cleansing' of the Temple by Jesus is described in Matthew 21.12-13, and Mark 11.15-16. The use of a whip of cords appears in John 2.13-16, though John places the whole incident at a Passover Feast towards the beginning of Jesus' public ministry.

Luke 22.14 records Jesus' longing to complete the Passover with his disciples.

John13.27 gives Jesus' dismissal of Judas from the Upper Room with the words, 'What you are going to do, do quickly.'

Letter 12

On the Greeks who came to see Jesus, and the link between the crucifixion and pagan mythology.

To Matthew, Son of Light, my beloved brother in the fellowship of Jesus, greeting.

Today some Greeks came to this town, and their coming put me in mind of an incident which had slipped my memory. Do you remember it? Some Greeks came to us in Jerusalem and asked specially to see the Master. They spent a long time with us, as I recall, and the Master seemed to find a strange significance in their visit. He asked them about Greek customs, and in particular about the gods they worshipped. The conversation got round to their god Adonis, and the Master showed particular interest in him. They spoke of this Adonis being born from a split myrrh-tree, I remember. The master seemed a little startled at this. I'd never seen him startled before, so I remarked it. He asked them particularly to repeat what they'd just told us. 'Adonis was born from a myrrh-tree,' they said. 'It was split by the blow of an axe, wielded by the father of the child.' There followed some fanciful tale about a king who seduced, or was seduced by (I don't remember which) his own daughter. But the master waved all that aside and again asked them to confirm the incident of the myrrh-tree. It seemed to have a special significance

59

for him, for he looked toward heaven and said in a very firm voice, 'Father, the hour is come!' The mention of myrrh seemed to be a sign to him. I wondered then what he meant. After the Greeks had gone, I heard him mutter, 'Myrrh, – the gift of death and the gift of love.' I didn't understand what it was all about at the time, but I have since begun to wonder whether your story of a gift of myrrh from a strange wise man at his birth might not have had something to do with it. I don't know where you got that tale from, but perhaps there is some truth in it. At any rate, the Master seemed much moved by the whole story of Adonis, as those Greeks told it. It seems that they believed he went down into the underworld for part of every year, because he had been protected in childhood by the god – or was it a goddess? – of the dead. He then rose again for the rest of the year, bringing new life to crops and so forth, because some other goddess (was it Aphrodite?) was either his mother or had caused his birth. The details of these Greek gods escape me, and are in any case irrelevant. Our Master pressed the Greeks on this subject of Adonis, and one of them – I think he was a merchant who had travelled in the East – said, 'Our Adonis is just like the Assyrian god Tammuz.' Then he explained that this Tammuz also is sent down into the underworld every year to rescue the crops from drought. They have a ceremony at which some poor man is actually sacrificed, and all the women weep 'for Tammuz' as he goes past to the place of execution. By the way, our own prophet Ezekiel knew of this custom, and deplored its occurrence in Jerusalem in his day. You probably know the passage.

Anyway, the visit of those Greeks to our Master was a turning-point for him, I'm convinced of it. He began to see that the sacrifice which he was already contemplating would be something the whole world could understand, if it was rightly presented and publicly carried out.

Which brings me back, Matthew, to my earlier insistence on getting the whole business onto a world-wide basis, and *not* making it an exclusively Jewish affair. The liberation opened up by our

Master's crucifixion is for all mankind. I have to admit here to a certain sympathy with that Saul – well, all right, Paul. He does seem to have grasped that all manner of Gentiles can believe, as well as us Jews. Anyone, yes anyone, who knows stories about dying in order to rise again and begin a new life can claim the Master's sacrifice as authentic. And though in ages to come men sprout wings to fly like birds, or – I'm being fanciful – though they come to be able to speak in Jerusalem and be heard in Jericho, so long as they believe in renewal of life by the way of death, our Master's name will live. If there's one piece of his teaching which is absolutely vital to me, it's the bit about seed being flung into the ground and dying in order to come to life. That, Matthew my brother, is a great truth, a universal truth and an everlasting truth. Make sure you stress it in your book!

My greetings to the followers of The Way who are with you. Thomas.

P.S. I was about to seal this letter when I remembered something else, which may relate to Barabbas. As I was reading the Scriptures a few days ago, I came across a passage in the Book of Leviticus which might interest you, as you continue to see the Master's life as a fulfilment of Scripture. It concerns two identical goats which were offered by Aaron the priest for the sins of Israel. One was sacrificed in the normal way to God. The other was led away into the wilderness to die. The first one was to 'make atonement' for the sanctuary itself, and for the altar. The second one was called the Scapegoat, and was seen as transporting away all the sins of the people Israel. You can find the passage for yourself, no doubt, and apply it if you wish to the Master and Barabbas, as the two goats. That might give a new depth to the great sacrifice as a sacrifice for Israel indeed, as well as for the pagan world. But for myself, I'm sticking to Purim as the festival at which our Lord was the victim, and to the Book of Esther as the background story.

Just a suggestion. T.

NOTES AND REFERENCES: LETTER 12

On the Greeks who came to see Jesus, see John 12.20ff, wherein also Jesus speaks of the grain of wheat falling to the ground and dying.

See Leviticus 16 for details of the sacrifice involving two goats.

Letter 13

Jesus' rejection of Kingship recalled, and related to the events of 'Palm Sunday'.

To Matthew, beloved brother in the Lord Jesus, grace, mercy and peace. All the saints here (you see I'm using the new term!) surround you with their prayers.

I am moved to take up again with you the matter of the 'Palm Branch' procession when we entered Jerusalem at Hanukah. Since I last wrote my old memory has been revolving round another incident from those blessed, but now so distant times. Do you recall a day when the Master had been teaching a great crowd, and when he had finished some of the rabbis came to him and begged him to declare himself openly as King of the Jews? He reacted more violently than anyone expected. 'No!' he cried, 'That I'll never accept!' and he turned his back on them and positively stormed away. We had to bundle up our few possessions quickly, as I recall, and run after him to catch up! It seemed to me at the time a really rude response to what was generously meant: a real offer of the crown of King David to the Master. But he was terribly agitated, and we actually had to flee from the scene. I can still hear the clamour of the crowd, 'Hosanna! Son of David!' growing ever more distant behind us.

I mention this because I'm convinced that our dear Master never for a moment wanted to be King. When he got onto the ceremonial donkey for the Procession of Palms, he can have had no intention whatever of throwing the Romans out of Jerusalem and claiming sovereignty. He was playing a ritual part in the established religious ceremony, to wit the part of Judas Maccabaeus in the annual Hanukah ritual. That's all he intended by it, Matthew. It simply does not fit in with his character to want to be a real King after the manner of David or Solomon. Remember how we were all so mistaken about that! I can still hear Simon asking, 'Lord, will you please now restore the Kingdom to Israel?' We all had that expectation of him, deep down, and we were all wrong. I think myself that he regarded kingship of any sort as a temptation of the Devil. Didn't he tell us of those days after his baptism, when he went into the desert alone to test his vocation? If I've got it right, one of the temptations he then faced was to seek political power. He regarded that as a temptation from the Devil himself. So when those rabbis offered him the crown, he fled from them as from Satan himself. It was abrupt, sudden, rude, almost as if the pit of hell had opened before him.

He wanted to rule, Matthew, but not as a king rules. He wanted to give his very life in service to the people. He wanted, and still wants, to take away all impurity, corruption and imperfection from our human nature. He wanted to bridge the great gulf of Sin that separates us all from God. He came to make us all Children of Light. That's why *we* call him 'Lord', Matthew. That's why all our converts here call him 'Lord'. That's why people still to come will call him 'Lord'. He rules only from and through the Cross. Tell the world that, Matthew, and the Lord prosper your writing.

The saints here send their greetings to you as one who companied with the Lord. Thomas.

NOTES AND REFERENCES: LETTER 13

For Jesus' refusal of kingship, see John 6.15.

For his refusal of earthly kingdoms, see the accounts of the Temptations in Matthew 4.8-10; Luke 4.5-8.

'Saints' as used in the New Testament signifies merely followers of Jesus, rather than people of peculiar holiness. See the introductions to many of St. Paul's epistles.

Letter 14

In which the slave Lychorida gives an account of the trial of Jesus.

To Matthew, beloved brother in the Lord, greetings. I pray that you may be kept steadfast in The Way, as by the grace of the Master I am myself.

I had scarcely put down my pen from writing the last letter when something happened which compels me to take it up again. There came to our little company of believers an elderly slave-woman. She had been taken prisoner as a child, together with her mother, and together they were sold to a member of the Sanhedrin in Jerusalem, one Eleazar. He must have been quite high in the hierarchy – I don't know the full details – but she caught my attention with her story about a sudden assembling of the Sanhedrin one night long ago in the house of Caiaphas. She said that she was roused from sleep by her master, and told to run to the houses of several prominent members, with the message, 'Judas of Kerioth has come. Come quickly!' You can imagine that I pricked up my ears at this, and asked her to repeat it, and to tell me anything else she remembered about that night. Her story is very revealing about our friend Judas. I took it down from her verbatim, but as her Greek isn't very good I've paraphrased it. Here it is.

Statement of the Slave Lychorida

'My Lord Eleazar said to me, "Run to these houses" (he listed three). "Wake our friends. Say to them, 'Judas has come. Come quickly'." I ran. The streets were dark. Most people were already asleep, but some were sitting up late for the Esther-Festival. I knocked on doors, and gave the message. The men hastened to put on their cloaks and make for Caiaphas' house. When I got back, my Lord Eleazar told me to come with him. I carried a lamp, and we too hurried to the house of the High Priest. There, several men who seemed to be important priests were already gathered. But one man, the one they called Judas, was held in the middle by two men, one on either side of him. They were clearly detaining him. He was pale with fear, shaking as if with a fever. They made him sit down to one side, and I was sitting right by him in the shadows. I heard him offer his guards money to let him go. "I must get back," he kept saying. They replied, "We need you in the garden. It's dark. You must identify the Rabbi for us. Be quiet!" They kept a firm grip on him, and wouldn't let him go. Meanwhile the others debated what should be done with Jesus when they arrested him. "Full court to try him at once," said one. Others said that would be illegal at night. Then Caiaphas himself said, "At this Roman spring festival, might not someone be sacrificed on behalf of the people of Israel?" That set them all talking excitedly. "Good thinking", "That'll please the governor", "A Jewish victim to take away the Emperor's weakness", "A Jewish Haman, for the people to gloat over". At that point, my lord Eleazar bade me run to the Captain of the Temple Guard, to bring soldiers to carry out an arrest. Then there was more running in the dark to do, to assemble the full Sanhedrin Court at night. I got back to Caiaphas' house exhausted, and hoped to doze off behind my lord Eleazar. But then I saw Jesus brought in. I knew him, for I had seen him in the Temple. My lord Eleazar had argued there with him. He didn't like Jesus, and wanted him dead. I was sorry about that, for I liked Jesus from the moment I set eyes on him. But I knew I'd get a beating if I said anything, so I held my tongue.

'I fell asleep while they tried Jesus there. I don't know what went on. A great shout woke me. "Blasphemy! Away with him at once to governor Pilate! Get a death warrant clapped on, and we'll have him as Haman! Then pass him to the Romans to do what they will with him!" By this time, dawn was beginning to break. We all hurried to Pilate's residence. Presently Pilate came out to us. I couldn't see much, standing behind lord Eleazar. A big crowd began to gather, because it was time to choose the two people for the Esther-festival, one to be Mordecai and live, the other to be Haman and die. My master was really quite a kind man, and explained it to me. He told me that both men were condemned to death, but that one would be released for a time. There was a longish delay while Pilate heard the case against Jesus. Then someone shouted, "If you don't give a death-warrant, you're no friend of Caesar." That seemed to decide things, and Jesus was put under sentence of death. Then another prisoner was brought out, for the crowd to choose between them. I heard a whisper that this other man was a murderer. He was put to stand beside Jesus. At once Lord Eleazar, and many other priests, began to move among the crowd. They whispered, "Choose the brigand for Barabbas, son of the Emperor-God!", "Choose the brigand for Mordecai", "Choose the brigand..." Often they'd slip money into people's hands to get them to do as they said. So when Pilate said, "Choose!" a great shout went up, "The brigand for Barabbas! Crucify that Jesus! Crucify him!" I felt very sorry for him. We left as they were tying him to a whipping post.'

So there you have it, Matthew my brother. It seems Judas was caught, kept against his will to identify the Master for the soldiers. But in the Providence of God it turned out that this made everyone think that it was a betrayal, as the Master himself had wished. Whether Judas really meant to slip back in to the supper party, or just to fade away quietly (more likely, I think), we'll never know. I even wonder if his sudden violent end by his own hand wasn't premeditated, to preserve the Master's own sacrifice from any remote taint of suicide. Anyway, make of it what you can. The sacrifice on the Cross is what really matters now. But I've always had a tender spot for Judas. He was a companion of The Way, and a dear friend. What happened to him is nothing less than a tragedy.

My chance meeting with this elderly slave-woman, now joyful in the freedom our Master gives, reminds me that something ought to be said about Mary of Magdala. She was very close indeed to our Master, particularly during those last weeks. I do recall that she seemed to realize before the rest of us that He was going to meet his end. Do you remember that she burst in on a supper we were having with a rich supporter, and anointed the Master's feet? I'm afraid I thought at the time that she was mad – that is, madder than usual. But for all her odd ways, she was very perceptive about some things, and the Master, I know was very fond of her. More than that I can't say, and wouldn't if I could. We all respected the Master's privacy in his relationship with her, and I believe we should keep it that way. But she should not be left out of the account, if only because that Master effected such an amazing change in her.

May the Lord continue his blessing on your labours. Greetings from the children of light around me. Thomas.

NOTES AND REFERENCES: LETTER 14

The accounts of the trial of Jesus are in Matthew 26.57ff; Mark 15; Luke 23 and John 18.19ff.

Caiaphas' remark that one man should die 'for the people' is in John 11.50, reaffirmed at John 18.14.

The anointing of Jesus is recorded variously in all 4 gospels: Matthew 26.6-13; Mark 14.3-9; Luke 7.36-50; John 12.1-8. None, however, state that it was done by Mary of Magdala (Mary Magdalene). In fact, John says that it was Mary of Bethany, sister of Martha and of Lazarus, who performed the act.

Scholars are divided as to whether the 'sinful woman' of Luke's account should be identified with Mary Magdalene, whom he mentions in the following chapter as one from whom Jesus cast out seven devils. There is also uncertainty about where the act took place. If indeed it was in Bethany, then St. John's identification of the woman with Mary of Bethany is very likely to be correct. But could the two Marys be the same person? Elsewhere in the Gospels, Mary Magdalene is noted as one of the women who followed with the disciples, who observed the Crucifixion from a distance, and who was the first to recognize the Risen Lord at the Resurrection. This close relationship to our Lord has given rise to further speculation as to whether Jesus was married to her.

The title 'Rabbi' could not properly have been ascribed to him if he were not married. In any case, an account of Jesus' life and work would be incomplete if it did not include reference to her.

Letter 15

A final letter, in which Thomas sets in order the events of Jesus' ministry, from the declaration at Caesarea Philippi to the crucifixion.

Greetings in the Lord Jesus, Master of all in Heaven and Earth, Lord of those who stand in the Light, to my brother Matthew. Grace and peace be to you and those with you who are fellow-disciples with us.

I am constrained to write to you this one letter, which must be the last I shall ever write to you about the matter of your book, unless the Lord ordains otherwise. The ways to India through the mountains are now open, and I look to depart within days. A train of merchants and scholars is even now assembling, and through my prayers I am assured that I must indeed go with them. As your work continues where you are (may God prosper it), there is really no point in my writing further. By the time letters from me could reach you, your book will already be finished and in circulation. Even now I know not whether my most recent letters have reached you.

So I'm sad, deeply sad, Matthew, that we shall in all probability never meet again in this life. May the Lord hasten the day of his coming! I must now set down for you a memorial of the days of our companying with the Master, in the order of the events as I recall them. For the order in which things happen is an expression of the providence of God. Only when a story is told in the proper order does it have its full effect. And

71

God was in and with our Master, of that I am absolutely certain, though it all took place as long as forty years ago (can it be?). Sometimes I still burst into song when I remember those days. How I positively danced alongside him, as he spoke the great truths of the Kingdom! Of course I was much younger then, scarcely past my Bar-Mitzvah when I joined the group. How the Master loved children! Do you remember when he set a child before us all, and said that we must all become as trusting and as innocent as children if we wanted to have a part in the Kingdom? I believed that, and believe it still. Perhaps that's why so many of our group were very young. But I digress. Forgive me: I am now old! I knew then, as I know daily still, that even were the Master to die, his presence could never depart from me. And how blessed was I when in that secret upper room I saw with my own eyes the wound in his side! Praise be to our risen Master, victorious over death and sin!

But to work. Time is short. First, I recall that his greatest teaching began, so far as I'm concerned, at Caesarea Philippi. It was there, you remember, that he first told us the dreadful truth: that he must go to Jerusalem and be killed. It hit us all with the force of a thunderbolt. And Peter spoke up for us all, saying that we would have none of it. But the Master insisted that we should go at least as far as Jericho. We were adamant that we would go no further. But as far as I recall, he was even then speaking of holding our next Passover in Jerusalem. Next, the message came that Lazarus was sick – remember Lazarus of Bethany? We couldn't refuse to go on to Bethany with him, for we knew his deep affection for Lazarus and all that household. From Bethany, Jerusalem is only a day's walk, so we were all, even then, getting a bit on edge.

The next event in the sequence, as I recollect, came with the approach of Hanukah, and with it the annual Judas Maccabaeus procession up to the Temple. I retain a vague memory of certain Elders, perhaps they were pilgrims going up for the feast, coming to see the Master. It may have been they who offered him the role of Judas Maccabaeus. We talked a lot about going into Jerusalem itself for the Feast, because it meant our going into the very Temple precinct itself. It was agreed that we would go with him, despite our fears and anxieties for his safety – and, be it said, our own. Once that was agreed, we left the details about arranging the ceremonial donkey, marshalling the procession and so on, to the Master and our most trusted friend, Judas.

Then came the big day. A huge crowd of pilgrims and citizens from the city assembled at the Mount of Olives, bringing their old palm-branches from last year's Feast of Tabernacles, as was the custom. Do you remember that entry into Jerusalem? Wasn't it simply terrific? When the Master began to set about the traders in the Temple and throw them out of it, I forgot all my fears. I was simply ecstatic. We must have known that it was bound to lead to trouble, but, speaking for myself, I had long since ceased to worry. From that moment on, the Master simply ruled on the Temple mount.

Next came our decision to withdraw to a safe house in the city. The Master's friends from Qumran found us that upper room that we were to get to know so well. We actually lived there for weeks, until the approach of the Festival of Purim in springtime. The Master taught daily in the Temple, while we all spoke about him to interested listeners and enquirers. We made a great team, didn't we, Matthew, you and I, building on what we'd done together when he sent us all out in pairs – wasn't that the previous year? Those were great days. We began to forget our fears for the Master, as he spoke to us about Purim and Passover. I recall feeling, 'This really is going to be a time of Liberation.' He spoke particularly about longing to celebrate that Passover with us. Aren't we lucky to have those two Festivals within a month of each other? It makes a month-long festival of Liberty for oppressed people everywhere.

So we got to Purim, or rather to the eve of it. He spoke to us of taking an active role in this ceremony also, by playing the part of Mordecai, our Jewish hero who rose from prison to such eminence in Babylon. We all fell for it, thought it was a wonderful idea, even though it meant his being taken temporarily into custody by the authorities. He was in such complete control of the Temple that we thought he could take over the City as well. Looking at it now, with hindsight, I know we must all have been in a state of self-delusion. But then we were all talking about the Messiah

and the coming Kingdom of God on earth. There was even some speculation as to which of us would be on his right hand and on his left when
the Kingdom came in! (I was pretty low on the list, I remember). I think
somebody did ask the Master how he proposed to be released from prison
to play the part of Mordecai. He said it was all being arranged, and we left
it at that. Myself, I simply assumed that the one doing the arranging was
once again our faithful Judas. Ah, those heady days! We felt so consumed
by Light that it was as if darkness couldn't exist!

So we came to supper together, in the upper room, never even imag-
ining that it would be our last. By this time the city was full of pilgrims,
coming pouring in for the double Festival. Those who weren't speaking
of Purim were speaking of Passover, and those who weren't speaking of
Passover were speaking of Purim. But I'll not forget that supper, if I live
to be the age of Methuselah. It was the shock announcement, 'There's
a betrayer in our midst,' that suddenly made everyone fall absolutely
quiet. He said it with a terrible gravity and sadness. I've never been able
to forget that announcement; he said it so deliberately, so intensely. He
meant us all to hear it. I believe he meant it specially for Judas. I think
now that he must have said it so that his own coming sacrifice might
have no taint of suicide attached to it. He was arranging with Judas to
have himself turned in to the authorities that very evening. It was delib-
erate on his part, but it must on no account appear so. It must be made
to look like betrayal. That was his final message to Judas, who, as I recall,
left shortly afterwards, before the meal was anything like over.

Next in order – the olive-garden at night. Matthew, do make a point
of how long we waited there. I know I fell asleep, and was only wakened
when the arresting party was on top of us. But I heard later that Peter,
James and John, who'd been specially asked to keep watch, fell asleep no
less than three times. When I woke, I noticed that the moon had moved
right over. Why did he wait so long, when we'd all expected to go out to
Bethany for the night? I still don't really know the answer to that. I expect
it was because the garden had been set with Judas as the rendezvous, and
we had to wait until the arresting party appeared. At the time, all I could
think of was running away in terror. But I have one more burning impres-

sion of those few moments before we all took to our heels. It concerns dear brother Judas. He came back to us just for a moment or two, embraced the Master in the usual familiar way, whispered something in his ear, and then disappeared in the darkness. I never saw him again. But I had a strange feeling, as I looked back on that incident, that it had been deliberately staged – that we were meant to see that last embrace. Perhaps it was because the Master stepped towards the lanterns: or did he embrace Judas until the men with the lights came rushing up? It was all so confusing. But that impression of the last kiss of greeting being deliberately staged has stayed with me all down the years, in a way which I can only describe as uncanny. Anyway, the Master was immediately taken into custody – though somebody did try to make a fight of it, for I recall a sword flashing in the moonlight, and the Master shouting 'Put that sword away! Use it, and you'll die by it!' I can't be more precise than that. It was dark, very dark. Terror seized me along with the rest, and my feet took me out of there almost before my head was properly awake.

After that, well, you are as well placed as I am to piece the story together. The Master was evidently taken to the house of Caiaphas, where some sort of trial took place. He was condemned, and taken to Pilate for sentencing at the Purim presentation of two prisoners. Our hopes that he would be released as the Mordecai for the year, the Roman 'Barabbas', were dashed. How could it have been otherwise? The priests saw to that, and the Master was taken away to the legionaries for their ghastly 'softening up' treatment.

Matthew, we must get this right, or the full significance of the Master's sacrifice will be lost. Saul's idea of it being Passover is good as far as it goes (though, God forgive me, I grudge him even that). But it doesn't go far enough. Our Master is the final Liberator, the Lord of all Festivals, Roman, Jewish or other. Blessed be his holy name for ever.

Now I must really put down my pen. May the victorious Master live with you as he does with me. May he lay his hand of blessing on you and your work. May your writing inspire thousands, to the Master's glory. Dwell ever in the Light. Grace, mercy and peace be yours, now and forever. Farewell. Your brother in the Lord, Thomas.

NOTES AND REFERENCES: LETTER15

For Methuselah, the legendary oldest man in the Bible, see Genesis 5.27.

The death and raising of Lazarus is recorded in John 11.

The accounts of Jesus' vigil in Gethsemane, and his arrest there, are in Matthew 26.36ff; Mark 14.32ff: Luke 22.39ff: and John 18.1-12.

The incident of the presentation of a child as a model of belief is in Mark 9.36: Luke 9.47.

Letter 16

A subsequent letter to the Apostle Paul, in which Thomas seeks forgiveness for his previous mistrust, and comes round to Paul's position on Passover.

Thomas, servant of the Lord of Light in India, to Paul, worthy and blessed servant of the same Lord Jesus, greetings. The prayers of the saints in this place continue for you, that your work may be abundant and fruitful in The Way.

May Jesus in his living power bless your endeavours, as even now he continues to bless mine. How our unworthiness is overcome by his grace! How our weakness is raised to power by his strength! Every day I see that grace and strength revealed, as men and women here raise their eyes from idols to worship the Lord of Life, our true Prince of Light.

My brother, this letter if it ever reaches you bears my plea for your forgiveness. You must know that for years I have suspected and even resisted your teachings. But the Lord has opened my eyes to see in you his own grace, and a wisdom which surely comes not from man alone, but from your experience of the risen Saviour. I too was raised from disbelief to faith, when I found among my fellow-disciples the risen Lord standing before me. If only we could meet, to share our experiences of recognizing the living Master! But I know this will never come to pass, this side of the tomb.

I experienced something of that same amazement as I read your letter to me. It came as the opening of the eyes to a blind man. It carried a power of conviction which I acknowledged at once as coming from the Spirit. So I now write, not only to thank you for your perception, but to bless the Lord for his wisdom revealed through it.

I would endorse – if my opinion matters – your vision of the way forward. The foundation of all is, as you say, Jesus crucified and risen. His new life pulses in our veins; his gracious way is our way of life. Nothing must detract from that sacrifice of his on the cross. It is done. It is done once and for all. No further sacrifice need ever be offered to God, for the sacrifice of Jesus is perfect. And so that nothing should besmirch that sacrifice, or take from it one jot of significance, the work of Judas must be seen forever as betrayal. The Master knew what Judas was doing, of that I have no doubt. But if he chose to call it 'betrayal' then that is what it was – though the Master himself connived at it. 'Betrayal' let it be, though Judas did only what the Master directed him to do. I was a friend of Judas, as we all were. I believe that when he took his own life, he did it to cover the Master's tracks, so that no least hint of 'planned death' should come near the Crucifixion. For planned death is suicide: and our Master's sacrifice was not suicide – not in any way.

Even so, my brother, your insistence on Jesus as 'our Passover' is right. Passover has the great story of the Exodus from Egypt, and Liberation, attached to it. Purim has only a tale of vengeance, the Jews killing their enemies as their enemies had planned to kill them. We can agree, can we not, that though the event took place at Purim, all the significance of Passover is attached to it and transmitted through it. The Master sets his seal on the struggle for our freedom. That struggle is best expressed in the Book of Exodus rather than the Book of Esther. So let Passover stand as our Feast of the Cross, and let Purim fade away. I can testify that our master longed to celebrate Passover in Jerusalem, even as Purim approached. So let us continue to fulfil that longing, and celebrate his cross as a Passover, even as you proclaim. I note that you very judiciously say that our last supper together took place 'on the night that the Master was betrayed', rather than making reference to any feast whatever.

I had not thought my old companion Matthew would show you my letters. How could I have written so harshly of you in them! But now my very blind opposition to you has produced a fruit of glory, in your wonderful letter of forbearance and understanding. My hope is that now Matthew will destroy my letters, lest anything else in them should call in question the Master's work. Should any of those letters now be in your possession, I beg you to destroy them at once, lest, falling into the wrong hands, they should detract in any way from the mighty sacrifice of our Master.

Yet there remains the matter of Barabbas. His release at the same time as our Master's condemnation points inescapably to the event taking place at Purim rather than Passover. I am almost ready to ask Matthew to delete all mention of him from the record – but not quite. The event actually occurred, and I believe it is now attested elsewhere than in Matthew's record. We cannot deny, and ought not to conceal, anything that has actually happened. It is within the Providence of God. I know not how this is to be resolved, and await further light on it.

I write this knowing that my time is now very short indeed. Not only are the posts from here extremely uncertain, but my natural span of life is more and more over-extended. I long to be with the Master again, in the fullness of his light. How blessed I was to be with him when he walked in Galilee! How much more to embrace him in the fullness of his Kingdom! The opposition to my teaching here grows stronger every hour, and I know there are many who would be glad to see the last of me.

Farewell, Paul, and may our gracious Master enfold you with his blessing. Thomas.

NOTES AND REFERENCES: LETTER 16

Thomas' conversion from doubt to belief in the resurrection of Jesus is recorded in John 20.24ff.

Paul's 'Damascus Road' conversion is in Acts 9.

Paul's description of the Last Supper, used today as part of many communion services in church, is in 1 Corinthians 11.23ff.

There is a strong possibility that Paul was in fact executed in Rome in 64 A.D., well before the imagined commencement of these letters.

LEGENDARY POSTSCRIPT:
THOMAS' DOUBTS RESOLVED

A curious result of Thomas' reputation for 'doubting' was the story that he had received the girdle of the Virgin Mary herself, after she had been taken up into heaven. A document described by the German scholar Tischendorf as 'of late complexion', and falsely attributed to Joseph of Arimathaea, gives an account of the Assumption into heaven of the body of the Virgin. Forewarned by an angel that she was soon to die, she sent for Joseph of Arimathaea and other disciples. Although the Apostles were widely scattered in their various missions, all were suddenly transported to her bedside on clouds – all except Thomas. She died, and after various miraculous interventions they took her body to the tomb. There such a blinding light shone about them that they did not see when her body was taken up to heaven, but assumed that it remained in the tomb where they had placed it. At that instant Thomas was transported to join them, and he alone saw the body being taken up to glory. 'Make your servant glad by your glory!' he cried, and Mary threw down to him her girdle. Then the disciples, discovering Thomas among them, began to reprove him for his sceptical ways. He told them what he had seen, but they refused to believe him, insisting that the body of the Virgin was still in the tomb. When he demonstrated that it was not, they begged his forgiveness, and he was re-instated fully into their fellowship. 'Behold, how good and joyful a thing it is for brethren to dwell together in unity,' is the pious conclusion of the author.

The incident of the Virgin's girdle is depicted in Renaissance portraiture, and is particularly celebrated in the Italian town of Prato. Whatever we may think of its fictional nature, it does serve to highlight for us the importance of Thomas and his doubts, so that we may reflect with St. John's Gospel, 'How blessed are those who have not seen, and yet believe.'

SUGGESTIONS FOR FURTHER READING

The Gospel of Thomas, translated and annotated by Stevan Davies: Darton Longman and Todd, 2003.

Judas: Images of the Lost Disciple, by Kim Paffenroth: Westminster John Knox Press, 2001, gives a useful conspectus of views of this mysterious disciple down the ages.

The New Testament Apocrypha in various editions contains many documents from the first and second centuries of the Christian Church. It shows that the concocting and circulating of curious (and spurious) stories about Jesus is of very ancient origin.

Among 'alternative' lives of Jesus being circulated today:

Jesus the Man, by the Australian scholar Barbara Thiering: Doubleday 1992; Corgi 1993. Based on the Dead Sea Scrolls and the activities of the Qumran community, this work views the Gospels as cryptic works requiring a technique known as 'Pesher' to translate them.

The Book that Jesus Wrote – John's Gospel, by the same author, (Corgi, 1998) is as radical as its title suggests.

Out of Egypt, by Ahmed Osman: Arrow Books, 1999, sees the roots of Christianity in ancient Egypt rather than in Palestine.

Jesus the Heretic, by Douglas Lockhart: Element Books, 1997, seeks to disentangle the actual teachings of Jesus from the interpretations put upon them by the disciples and by Paul.

Alongside such works as these may be placed the solid orthodoxy and immense scholarship of John Dominic Crossan, whose work *The Historical Jesus* (Harper Collins, 1992) will long remain standard.

The Gnostic Gospels by Elaine Pagels: Vintage Books, 1981, gives a useful, readable and scholarly insight into the Nag Hammadi discoveries and Gnosticism in general.

Liberating the Gospels by John Shelby Spong: (Harper San Francisco, 1996). An interpretation of the four Gospels and Acts as dependent on Jewish midrashic practice.

Relevant mythological works must include Frazer's classic *The Golden Bough*, particularly the parts entitled 'The Dying God' and 'The Scapegoat'. Note also the critique of Frazer by Andrew Lang in *Magic and Religion*.

A Prayer

O blessed Saint Thomas,
twinned with us in doubt and scepticism;
take our wavering hands
and lay them in the Master's side,
that our uncertainty may be turned to faith,
and our faith made stronger by our doubt,
so that in our life we too may reflect
the living presence of the Son of Man.
Amen.